Mad Women in Romantic Writing

Philip W Martin

Senior Lecturer in English
King Alfred's College, Winchester

THE HARVESTER PRESS · SUSSEX
ST. MARTIN'S PRESS · NEW YORK

First published in Great Britain in 1987 by
THE HARVESTER PRESS LIMITED
Publisher: John Spiers
16 Ship Street, Brighton, Sussex
and in the USA by
ST. MARTIN'S PRESS, INC.
175 Fifth Avenue, New York, NY 10010

British Library Cataloguing in Publication Data
Martin, Philip W.
Mad women in romantic writing.
1. English literature — History and
criticism   2. Mental illness in literature
3. Women in literature
I. Title
820.9′353   PR409.M4
ISBN 0-7108-0697-3

Library of Congress Cataloging-in-Publication Data
Martin, Philip W.
Mad women in romantic writing.

Bibliography: p.
Includes index.
1. English literature—19th century—History and
criticism.   2. Mental illness in literature.
3. Women in literature.   4. Romanticism—England.
5. Psychoanalysis and literature—Great Britain.
I. Title.
PR469.M47M34   1987   820′.9′353   87-20678
ISBN 0-312-01246-2

Typeset in 11 pt Plantin by
C. R. Barber & Partners (Highlands) Ltd.,
Fort William, Scotland
Printed in Great Britain by
Billing and Sons Ltd, Worcester

For Lynne, Christopher, Roly and Toby

Contents

List of Illustrations   viii
Preface   ix

Introduction   1

1. Writing Woman's Madness   14

2. Mad Women in Romantic Psychiatry   28

3. Bereavement, desertion and decay: Wordsworth's deranged women and the fractured family   49

4. Secret Lives: *Sense and Sensibility*, *The Bride of Lammermoor*, *Wuthering Heights*, *Great Expectations*   92

5. Different Desires: *Jane Eyre* and *Wide Sargasso Sea*   124

6. Freud's Short Stories: Tales of Excessive Desire   140

Appendix: Case Studies   169

Select Bibliography   192
Index   195

Illustrations

Plate 1
Johann Heinrich Füssli, *Mad Kate* (1806-7)

Plate 2
Henry Fuseli, *Woman with a Stiletto, Man's Head with a Startled Expression* (1810-20)

Plate 3
Francis Danby, *Disappointed Love* (1821)

Preface

In a little-known sketch by Henry Fuseli, a woman is represented holding a stiletto in her right hand and a leg, probably of a deer, in her left. Her face wears an expression of manic delight. An inscription on the sketch in an unknown hand reads 'Mary Anne Lamb', and if she truly in Fuseli's subject here, then the drawing effects the only real entry of Romanticism's most famous madwoman into its art. For if the spectre of Mary Lamb's madness haunts the period, it remains for the most part in a realm distinct from that of its texts, which are concerned to present their madwomen as casualties of frustrated desires and broken promises, and not as creatures of dangerous frenzy. And so a cordon of silence is constructed around that dreadful incident of 1796, which nevertheless, in retrospect, bears a resonant symbolic relation to a subject common in the literature of the period and beyond. Fuseli breaks this ring of silence, and in representing Mary Lamb as a Maenad (this is the significance of the dismembered deer) effects a breach of Romantic decorum. Here the deranged woman stands as a creature of dark ritualistic power, not a casualty at all, and her mania inspires not pity, but terror, exemplified in the barely discernible, appalled male face behind her.

Such variations in convention are rare, and the endeavour of this book is to probe the strength of the orthodoxy which makes them so. In so doing, I hope to disturb the complacency with which I believe the madwoman is commonly received as an innocent literary subject, for what makes Fuseli's drawing so exceptional needs to be explained.

My academic debts are numerous. This study originated in a projected article on Wordsworth, and owes its inception to ideas found in James Averill's *Wordsworth and the Poetry of Human Suffering*. I am indebted to his scholarship and insight. Without the editors of the Cornell *Wordworth* and their scrupulous annotations and introductions, Chapter 3 could not have been written. Marjorie Levinson generously allowed me to see part of the typescript of her recent book on Wordsworth before publication, and while my methodology is less precise in formulation, it owes much to her fine example.

I thank those colleagues and students who have taken an interest in my work over the last five years. The English department at King Alfred's College has been most supportive. In particular, Dr John Simons has been unstinting in giving time and valuable advice, and these gifts, together with his friendship, have pulled me through the more difficult periods.

Dr David Jarrett and the students and staff of the Polytechnic of North London have twice provided stimulating forums for my work, for which I am very grateful. My thanks are also due to Howard Cooper, Margaret Hamer, Dr Carol Miles, Dr Christopher Mulvey and Charles Page. I thank my wife, Lynne, for her patience and tolerance.

I am indebted to the generous assistance of the library staff at King Alfred's College Library, Winchester, the Library of the Wellcome Institute, London, the London Library, and the Bodleian Library.

Introduction

This book is about a myth of women's madness, a myth not confined to the Romantic era or style, but one which found itself repeated in many texts to which the label can be applied. The myth tells a simple tale: the woman is left or found alone, a widow, a bereaved mother, a deserted wife or a jilted lover. Her mind is vulnerable to the disturbances caused by an obsession with past happiness or promises, perhaps an excessive desire for the lost object of her love. In some cases this disturbance leads to insanity and eventually even death. In others it leads to physical illness, fever or derangement. For the purposes of this book, 'mad' is used in its loosest sense to refer to the range of mental conditions in which what is accepted as normal behaviour is suspended or disrupted. It is difficult to rid the term of its pejorative implications, for the idea of madness has accumulated around it a mass of prejudices and fears which spring from the desire to keep the social fabric (as evinced in behaviour and conduct) intact. I use the term therefore as a means of referring to these anxieties, through which I may establish contact with the historical conditions of my texts without participating in their judgements, censorious or otherwise.

In medical terms, the malady with which I am chiefly (but not exclusively) concerned was often referred to as erotomania, a term well established in the language of English medicine as early as 1640, when Edmund Chilmead published his translation of a French work, *De la maladie d'amour, ou melancholie érotique*, by Jacques Ferrand (Paris, 1623) and titled it *Erotomania*.[1] Referring most usually to

I

disappointment in love, erotomania received an increased amount of attention towards the end of the eighteenth century. Erasmus Darwin spoke of it in his influential *Zoonomia* (1794) as a disease most often suffered by women, and Thomas Arnold, writing in 1806 and making reference to Darwin's classifications of insanity, decided that there were a number of kinds of 'pathetic insanity' in which 'some passion is in full and complete possession of the mind', among which he numbers 'amorous insanity' and 'bashful insanity', this latter originating in concealed love and often resulting in 'that dreadful kind of insanity the *furor uterinus*'. Thomas Trotter, writing at almost the same time, sees woman's nervous diseases as deriving most commonly from 'long-protracted grief' or 'disappointed love'.[2] A fuller account of these writings and the tradition to which they belong will be found in Chapter 2, and examples of their case-studies comprise the Appendix.

It is not the purpose of this study to diagnose Romantic literature's mad or deranged women by way of the medical classifications current in the period. That would be a far more specialist enterprise. While the second chapter brings forward what I have taken to be a representative selection of works debating woman's madness, this body of material is not assumed to be immediately transferable to the conditions and behaviour witnessed in novels and poems. There was no very full consensus on the causes or diagnoses of woman's derangement (although some positive directional shifts are identifiable) and additionally, I have not been able to assume that the novelists and poets with whom I deal were acquainted with contemporary medical works.[3] It is nevertheless possible to place the deranged and mad women studied in this book within a distinct psychiatric tradition dating from the Romantic period and usually associated with the name of Philippe Pinel. Pinel's place in the history of medicine is usually emphasized by reference to his monumental act of freeing the patients at the Salpêtrière and the Bicêtre from the instruments of restraint, an action that is equally often interpreted as equivalent in significance to the storming of the Bastille in ushering in a new post-revolutionary age. Foucault has disputed this interpretation and its ramifications in some detail.[4] However the symbolic meanings of Pinel's action are established, it still indicates one important emphasis in the understanding of insanity in the Romantic period: the diagnosis that prefers to locate madness in the imbalance of the passions, in behavioural and historical causes, and will treat it not by repression and restraint, but by finding ways of redressing the equilibrium by changing the environment. Thus both sanity and insanity depend upon 'the emotional factors in mental experience',[5] an aetiology which combines with the common assumptions about woman's sensibility to offer her up as a particularly susceptible victim.

I take this to be a full and positive shift into Romantic psychiatry, with clear parallels in contemporary socio-political writings.[6] Nevertheless, this leaves us with a genealogy of Romantic madness that may be too indistinct for convenience. Pinel's historical significance must be located in his recommendations for treatment and their implications, and not in his mapping of the physical causes of madness. For although Pinel makes a conceptual break with the Lockean understanding of insanity, his models still carry traces of the medicine of the humours, Aristotelian structures of the balanced passions, and they are caught up therefore with earlier notions of melancholy and enthusiasm that were widespread in the seventeenth and eighteenth centuries.[7] Whatever his models for the conversions of emotional trauma into mental disturbance and the genealogical confusions which attend them, Pinel's new therapeutic methods thrust the study of emotional history into the foreground, and in this respect, the parallels established with Romantic writing are strong. For the impulse I am investigating here is that which centres on the woman's madness being a consequence of her private and sometimes her secret emotional life, and in literature it is a shift that might be exemplified by reference to Cowper and Wordsworth. For Cowper, crazy Kate is a sentimental motif, a decorative and quaint object in the landscape. In Wordsworth, the same figure is the subject of historical and biographical interest, even (as in the case of Martha Ray) when that interest remains frustrated. This example has all the usual liabilities of convenience, but this search for the origins of madness, and their consequences for the present, are features of all the works I discuss.

There may have been nothing new, then, in Pinel's insistence (or that of many English writers of the same period) that madness was primarily an emotional condition, but the prominence given to this judgement by the publicity accorded to the new therapeutic treatments and the institutional regimes which grew up around them,[8] are sufficiently consequential features of a material history to allow us to speak with confidence of a new psychiatry. It is in the context of this new psychiatry that Romanticism is able to combine its own new interest in individual psychology with the old mythologies of woman's weakness to produce the deranged women of its literature. These are not merely the new objects of a new repertoire. In the eighteenth-century literature of sensibility, such women may have served simply as indexes for the demonstration of individual sympathy: the personae or narrators using them as subjects provoking a response in which their own capacity to feel operated as a prime concern. The Romantic artist or protagonist proceeds a stage further: while sharing the affective response, she or he demonstrates the desire to understand the conditions and history of madness. The objective is now increased knowledge, a search for origins in which woman's derangements assume a critical place as part of the new view of the essential conditions of humankind or social life (Wordsworth and Freud), or a search for knowledge confined to the world of the novel, in which the woman's madness has to be known by the protagonist in the progress of his or her development (Charlotte Brontë, Jean Rhys, Dickens). Alternatively, or sometimes in combination with these formulae, woman's derangement serves to set up a contest with the conditions of normal social expectations, either to enforce what is desirable according to the text's centralised values (madness as deviance) or to disrupt or challenge commonly accepted norms (Scott, Jane Austen, Emily Brontë).

As will be seen, Romantic writing is used here as a term covering a variety of texts that in some respects are not usually found nestling together with much comfort, but in which may be found a number of Romantic characteristics: the writer as seer and harbinger of truth; the search for origins and causes; the significance of individual history as a complex of social and psychological interaction; the heightened role of feeling and emotional extremities in experience; a sustained interest in life's casualties and socially alienated groups or individuals; the place of suffering in the pathway to knowledge. I am well aware that any one of these characteristics may be claimed by other literary movements or styles, but I am not attempting to homogenize the writings here considered under the umbrella of Romanticism, so much as to trace selectively what I have chosen to see as a Romantic impulse, the investigation of the deranged woman's suffering and history.

This is a selective study for other reasons too, and some readers may be disappointed by the examples chosen. This book could have been about Yeats's Crazy Jane, Madame Bovary's hysterical fits, the breakdowns in *Villette*, or madwomen outside the Romantic or realist traditions: Ophelia, Lady Macbeth, or the deserted and crazed lovers of folk-balladry. Further, it could have been concerned to relate madness in literature to specific historical conditions, or to the history of psychiatric practice and institutional care. I would like to make the common protests about time, space and specific interests, but some further justification is necessary. Likewise, some statements may be rightly expected on this study's entry into territory already occupied by a feminist debate.

I have already indicated the nature of the Romantic interest. This established, women may be seen to occupy a particularly crucial area. While there are mad men in Wordsworth's poetry (for example) and in the tradition of sentimental literature which I have taken to be of formative influence, and while too, moving to the other end of my study, there is Freud's celebrated and much-debated study of male hysteria, in neither case does man's derangement become so central a concern in the development of the author's work. A retrospective view of psychoanalysis will see Freud's early studies of hysteria as the beginnings of practical analysis wherein a number of the essential concepts of Freud's work were starting to take shape. These studies of woman's derangement and illness in the context of a personally revealed history, to be extracted and explicated, can be seen as the birth of a new science. Similarly, an historical account of Wordsworth's poetry will notice the recurrent interest in the mad woman over and above the interest in the mad man, from the *Salisbury Plain* poems through the *Lyrical Ballads* and eventually into *Guilt and Sorrow*. In the cases of the novels I have chosen to discuss, there is a less remarkable authorial or thematic interest, but a heavy dependence, nevertheless, on the figure of the mad woman as a device governing the organization or rhetoric of the text. I have found no mad men to rival Bertha Mason or Miss Havisham in this respect. The repetition of the myth of woman's instability occurs regularly in the poetry and fiction of the nineteenth century, producing women who are not always mad, but metamorphosed through some pathological weakness: Wilkie Collins's woman in white, Hardy's Eustacia Vye, Bram Stoker's vampiric women, the confined figures of Tennyson's poetry. Here, then, are a number of conspicuous if apparently accidental reasons why women rather than men should become the focus in studying insanity and derangement in nineteenth-century writings. There may be some explanation of these coincidences in the rhetorical structures which ultimately govern and construct the cultural meaning of insanity. Madness is still commonly defined as the antithesis of reason. According to Foucault, this began in the eighteenth century as a newly secularized conception, and by 1780, the rough starting-point of this book, this would have been well established. Madness thus gives meaning to reason and finds itself easily allied to woman in the system of difference which grants self-justifying presence to a specifically partriarchal normality. This argument is developed in Chapter 2.[9]

The choice of novels here is also dictated by their common if not fully consistent use for woman's derangement. They do not repeat an identical formula in each case, but use the afflicted woman as a means of organizing and defining a centralized moral code. This code may or may not receive explicit articulation, but either way, it is the burden of the text's ideological project. I believe this to have been too frequently overlooked in the extant readings of these works, and it is my endeavour therefore, to twist the texts around to centralize the role of woman's madness in their rhetoric. Studies of *Jane Eyre*, for example, note correspondences between Jane and Bertha, but rarely concern themselves with the significance of Bertha's precise relation to the heroine. Accordingly most readers (in my experience) are likely to overlook the textual details which explain that her madness is not merely hereditary. By focusing on Bertha I have tried to skew the novel into a position open to a different perspective, without contorting it. Jean Rhys's *Wide Sargasso Sea* effects a similar re-orientation, and perhaps this is the place to say that it is included here not so much as a Romantic work, but as a profound reading of a Romantic myth.

This book enters an area in which a number of feminist writers are already active, but it is not a feminist book for the rather banal reason (which some may find naive) that its writer is a man. Many of the techniques of reading employed here have origins in feminist theory and practice, and as such this study engages with the activities of women's studies, but it does not attempt to colonize a space that is not its own. In this respect, it reflects something of my teaching experience, wherein I am conducting seminars with groups largely comprising women. Not to participate in feminist discourse in such situations would be perverse, but to co-opt it in the form of closed readings would be dangerous. This book attempts to open readings therefore, frequently more than one of the same text, and there is another way in which it reflects my recent teaching in that it attempts to work between theory and pragmatic interpretative reading. The predominant method employed may be labelled close reading (but not practical criticism) and within this method I have called on a limited but diverse range of strategies deriving from theory to elucidate my subject.[10]

As the title indicates, the subject of this book is writing, and not specifically literature, history or ideology. The emphasis is on the accumulations and displacements of meanings which issue from the rhetoric of writing women's madness, although I have sometimes accepted opportunities to relate the myths of woman's madness to ideological or institutional

structures.] The place of this myth as a trope in the wider
rhetoric of the text then, is the main concern, a concern that
engenders the dismantling of the apparatus of codes and
meanings that have assembled themselves around a subject
which may initially appear to be no more than a motif. Few
motifs are innocent however, and in the process of examining
this one, two interpretative possibilities come into play more
than any other. In their most diluted form they may be
outlined as follows.[The representation of woman's madness
may be taken as indicative of a familiar ideological
assumption in which her weakness is also a folly, her lack of
reason a symptom of her lack of 'masculine' control and
responsibility] If such a proposition emerges from the act of
reading,then it runs the risk of locking the text into the
ideology of its period, causing us to note yet another feature in
the history of patriarchy perhaps, a history realized in static
frames. Within this kind of reading,there is still much more to
be said, but its basic assumption about the placing of the text
in history (and the nature of that history) remain relatively
constant. Alternatively, woman's madness may be read in
such a way as to break up the ideological snare, for a reversal
of the rhetorical thrust which characterizes the woman as
unreason effects a disruption of the familiar values which
cluster around it, and her['unreason' may now be read as a
refusal to enter the world of patriarchal normality, a form of
radical protest, not necessarily self-initiated or self-aware.] In
other words,[the circuits may be reversed so that madness
may be seen as the positive quantity in the equation which
sets it against reason;] the punitive or habitual pejorative
connotations are shed, and the meanings produced in the act
of reading are re-organized accordingly. This disruptive
reading derives from the deconstructionist account of
logocentrism   (or   the   feminist-deconstructionist
phallogocentrism)[11] and the structure of supplementary
relations described by Derrida, but it is also [the tendency
present in Jean Rhys's reading of *Jane Eyre*,] which I shall
argue, does not contort the text but uses the instability of its
rhetorical procedure to produce a similar reversal. I have
used both interpretative strategies in this book, sometimes
concurrently, sometimes offering the advantages of one

against the other, and both seem to me to be perpetual possibilities. In the case of Wordsworth's poetry, the texts seem to stretch themselves into late eighteenth-century history and its well-documented events, and here I have been willingly pulled towards historicism and a fascinating manuscript history. When looking at *Jane Eyre*, conversely, I found the oppositional relations between Bertha and Jane a more powerful pull than that of history, and accordingly, I concentrate here on textual structure. The advantage of the disruptive reading may well consist in its liberating the reader from the position of reading 'as a man', for the refusal to see the text only as an object of ideological construction enforces at the same time a shift of stance wherein no related ideological assumptions of the present may interfere. The disadvantage of this reading strategy is in its potential underrating of history. This of course, is a continuing debate, and while I recognize that the two approaches are likely to divide themselves as preferences, I do not see that they are mutually exclusive.

Consequently, I have reserved the right to deflect into history, yet not, I ought to say, history as social and political events. The liability of this kind of study is that in accepting woman's derangement as a myth recycled through different but related conventions of writing, it may cause an eclipse of the real by the mythical. In other words, by concentrating on writing (though not exclusively) as a largely self-enclosed and self-reflexive activity, I do not have to confront the issue of how literature's mad women relate to real mad women. As an adjunct of this, some readers may believe that I do not believe in the material reality of woman's madness at all. This is not so. I have simply preferred not to venture into areas that cannot be my concern: the veracity or otherwise (for instance) of nineteenth-century theories of puerperal mania, or the relations between menstruation and other forms of derangement. While a political cause can be recognized in an attempt to demystify conventional accounts of woman's frailty, such a cause would not be freely embraced by feminists who take the essential differences of woman's biology as the first stage of any radical reassessment. This argument is one in which I cannot participate, and following

this, I make no judgements about whether or not women are
more likely to become deranged than men in 'real life' or
material history, however it is reconstructed. My subject is
madwomen in writing.

As for the precise relations of the madwomen in the
writings presented here and the mad women found in the
asylums of the nineteenth century, that is a relation I have
chosen not to pursue, largely because of the blurred nature of
any conceivable map which could site the relative positions
of text, material history, author and readership. Chapter
2, nevertheless, takes as its subject a documentary review of
the writings about women's madness that grew out of
institutional confinement, and occasional tentative compari-
sons are made between these writings and the literary texts.
Reality's ghost still intrudes however in the cases of those
texts which propose for themselves a factual matrix.
Wordsworth, for example, insistently notes that he or his
close friends have encountered very similar or identical
madwomen to those he writes about, and we know too that the
rural lunatics of late eighteenth-century England were
probably quite common features of country life, since they
were more liable to wander the perimeters of communities
than be confined. Scott conducts an elaborate editorial
procedure in *The Bride of Lammermoor* to attribute historical
authenticity to the events of his plot, and Dickens' Miss
Havisham was based on a London character that many of his
public may have been familiar with. Freud (for obvious
reasons) makes authentic claims for the experiences of his
hysterical women, yet finds the fictional form of the short
story the most persuasive mode to enforce the material reality
of the personal history on which so much depends. The kind
of literature studied here is often veracious in tendency if not
in technique, making claims for its fidelity to real life
sometimes through the chosen mode, sometimes through
footnotes or other annotations, or less directly, by taking
models from observed or reported facts.

However these works exhibit their claims for authenticity,
they do not reflect a material history so much as the complex
reactions between the inherited conventions of writing and
their authors' lived or imagined relations to the world. This

much I would certainly accept, and in this sense they are the documents of a material past, allowing a perceived relation between writings and the society which produced and consumed them. This is not the evidence of 'the real' but the evidence of what was thought to relate to the real in authentic terms, built around literary strategies deriving from and relating to lived relationships and the ideas that those relationships propagate. 'Attitudes to women' therefore, are to be found here, but are to be extracted with care from the complex of the text.[12]

It may also be the case that the presence of a definite assumption about woman's nature can be discerned in a model which sees the myth of her madness deriving from a form of displacement. This argument applies largely to Wordsworth's writings and the popular poetry of the late eighteenth century exploiting the madwoman as a subject. In these texts (and some others) the woman's madness is presented as the natural consequence of her desertion, and the muth thus established implies that women cannot survive in a normal or sane state without the protection of husband or lover. Yet it is also the case that deserted women of this period suffered great deprivation because of their economic insecurity, and what we may be witnessing, therefore, is the displacement of this material history into a mythical formula that prefers to assign this suffering to the congenital weakness of woman. The process of this displacement may actually be charted in the development of Wordsworth's poetry, as I shall argue in Chapter 3 (and its tensions may be evident in a single text, that of The Ruined Cottage). It is evident, too, in nineteenth-century medical and psychiatric writings, wherein madness is often seen in the context of extreme poverty, yet apparently without cognizance of any causal link.

To chart precisely the process by which this displacement operates is impossible. As in the cases of other parallels and connections which this book's material suggests, the suspected relationship may be a real one, but also may be justly described as of 'too magical a kind to be very amenable to analysis'.[13] In accepting Foucault's sceptical view that syntheses of movements or 'spirits' achieved by noting common factors are too frequently accorded 'unqualified,

spontaneous value'[14] I accept that my own challenge to the
values so often rehearsed in the name of Romanticism
(justice, liberty, sympathy) might run the risk of establishing
an alternative but equally artificial synthesis in its stead. I
have tried to avoid this by declining temptations to make
connections between my texts, and I must emphasize that no
'alternative' Romanticism is here being proposed. Rather,
this book sets out to investigate one small portion of the
history of the insane, and one small portion of the history of
womankind, combining here in a nexus that is established
through habits or conventions of writing governed by a
Romantic aesthetic or impulse.

Notes

1. See Richard Hunter and Ida Macalpine, *Three Hundred Years of Psychiatry 1535–1860* (London, 1963), p. 118. In his introduction, Ferrand apologized for writing 'of this subject, after so many, and so learned Physicians . . . have done so before.'
2. Erasmus Darwin, M.D., *Zoonomia; or, the Laws of Organic Life*, 2 vols (London, 1794), II, 363. Thomas Arnold, M.D., *Observations on the Nature, Kinds, Causes, and Prevention, of Insanity*, second edition, 2 vols (London, 1806), I, 185–7. Thomas Trotter, *A View of the Nervous Temperament*, second edition (London, 1807), pp. 85, 87.
3. Certain facts may be established. We know that Wordsworth read Hartley and Darwin for example, and Dr Sally Shuttleworth's research on Charlotte Brontë (as yet unpublished) reveals an acquaintance with medical and psychiatric works.
4. See Michel Foucault, *Madness and Civilization. A History of Insanity in the Age of Reason*, translated by Richard Howard (London, 1971). Foucault argues persuasively that the new humanitarianism was effectively a different kind of oppression.
5. Kathleen M. Grange, 'Pinel and Eighteenth-Century Psychiatry', *Bulletin of the History of Medicine*, 35 (1961), 442–53.
6. I am thinking here of the shifts towards environmental determinism in the work of Godwin particularly.
7. See Grange (1961); George M. Rosen, 'Emotion and Sensibility in Ages of Anxiety: A Comparative Historical Review', *American Journal of Psychiatry*, 124 (1967), 771–84; Vieda Skultans, *English Madness: Ideas on Insanity 1580–1890* (London, 1979).
8. The Retreat at York, set up by the Quaker community in 1796 and publicized in Samuel Tuke's *Description of the Retreat* (1813) was

widely recognized as exemplifying the new progressive modes of treatment. For a full-length study, see Anne Digby, *Madness, Morality and Medicine* (Cambridge, 1985).

9. See p. 42, and note 45.
10. Most relevant here is Foucault's work on the relations of power and Barthes on myth. See Foucault (1971) and his *Discipline and Punish: The Birth of the Prison*, translated by Alan Sheridan (Harmondsworth, 1977); *The Birth of the Clinic: An Archaeology of Medical Perception*, translated by A. M. Sheridan (London, 1976); Roland Barthes, *Mythologies*, translated by Annette Lavers (London, 1973). Derrida's *différance* and his notion of the nature of supplementary relations has also been influential in pointing the way towards developing disruptive readings. See Jacques Derrida, *Of Grammatology*, translated by Gayatri Chakravorty Spivak (Baltimore and London, 1976).
11. See Jonathan Culler, *On Deconstruction* (London, 1983).
12. The subject of this paragraph of course, is ideology, a term fraught with difficulties, and in attempting to move away from a crude model proposing homogeneous social thinking, I am drawing on the work of Gramsci and more significantly Althusser to form the alternative model suggested here. See Louis Althusser, 'Marxism and Humanism', in *For Marx* (Harmondsworth, 1969), p. 233.
13. Michel Foucault, *The Archaeology of Knowledge*, translated by A. M. Sheridan Smith (London, 1972), p. 21.
14. Ibid., p. 22.

CHAPTER ONE

Writing Woman's Madness

The village idiot, most commonly male and harmless, has a confirmed place in the western cultural tradition. His antics are the source of gentle derision, his lunacy close to the madness, and the wisdom beyond madness, that characterize the fool. Solitary, his presence is nevertheless accepted by the immediate community, and his alienation is of an incomplete kind. His difference is not essential: it partakes of the order which uses him to define its normality.

A similarly secure place may be found for the inspired madman whose derangement is the evidence of divine intervention. Moved in his ravings beyond the common bounds of knowledge and awareness, he mutters terrible truths about the world he inhabits, truths which ultimately locate this madness as the centre of real values. Such a figure, common enough in the Renaissance and beyond, bears the evidence of a disease betokening cultural health, and in this respect he is not unlike Focault's leper, who, even while being dragged backwards out of the church which forbids return, is told of the special grace of leprosy, the grace that secures punishment on earth, and thereby, a blessed state in the hereafter.[1] Yet this figure may also be Plato's madman: in the *Timaeus* prophetic and endowed with vision, in the *Phaedrus* led through suffering and penance to sacred completion. King Lear is the obvious example.[2]

The female lunatic is assigned a very different role. Her eccentricity is less easily tolerated, and finds no established place in the history of comedy. Far from being accused of an idiocy that lies somewhere beyond ignorance, seldom credited with the fool's perceptions, she is more usually condemned by being in possession of a dangerous knowledge or desire. Her abnormal behaviour is but a symptom, and the cherished mystery of femininity is preserved in the act of social excommunication that speaks of deep anxiety and fear.

Woman's madness in the western tradition is not always of this kind. Cassandra, it has been well noted, is an important archetype of the prophetic wisdom with frenzy.[3] Probably the strength of her presence ensures the fragmented survival of woman's power in madness in such figures as Ophelia, or even Wordsworth's mad mother. Yet it is also the case that woman's madness is less comfortably used in this tradition, first because of the interpretative prejudice which is constantly concerned to set man's fortitude and rationality against woman's lack of control, typically realised in such moments as this:

> When we entered, we found Socrates just freed from his fetters, and Xanthippe his wife – you know her – close to him, holding one of his children in her arms. As soon as she saw us, she began to wail and lament, as women are wont to do: 'O Socrates, here are your friends, come to look on you for the last time, and you on them!' And Socrates, looking at Crito, said, 'Crito, let somebody take her home;' so some of Crito's servants took her away, crying aloud and beating her breast.[4]

This is only half the story, however. The second reason, probably underlying the first, is that woman's madness is not open to the free interpretation play which is able to see man's madness as a metonym implying the presence of higher truth, or alternatively as a metaphor for deep inspiration. For woman's madness is constantly being closed down by the ubiquitous presence of hysteria. It is ever subject to a diagnosis which bears the formidable stamp of 'authenticity' declared in the name of medicine. Hysteria thus eclipses the positive possibilities of madness which are intercepted at source by the analysis which insists on secularizing the woman's derangement, on tying it to a physical disorder, explaining it by way of the peculiar actions of the uterus. And thus it is that medical discourse has inscribed into its history a structure that creates behavioural patterns which accord to sexual difference, and literary traditions have absorbed that structure. Although the sequence of medical writings from the earliest records to Freud is punctuated by attempts to distinguish between insanity and hysteria, the two are almost constantly in propinquity, even in the process of distinction, and this closeness establishes an interpretative formula that lends itself only too readily to free application when woman's madness is subjected to diagnosis.

The ancient Egyptians decided that woman was prone to special behavioural disorders on account of the fact that the uterus, a strange creature within a creature that was therefore strange, was liable to wander around the body, and the assumptions proceeding from this assertion have dogged medical theory and practice for the best part of four thousand years.[5] The shorter tradition of western literature has a different kind of continuity, but has carried along with it a mythology of womankind built upon a foundation that is ideologically very close to this fundamental premise of woman's medicine. Literature's uses for mad and deranged women are varied, but not as varied as one might initially expect, and what is particularly surprising is the regularity with which one diagnosis of the woman's disorder recurs. This analysis is not always explicit, sometimes remaining hidden within the sub-text, but its presence is ubiquitous: woman's madness, hysteria and abnormality are the result of the deprivation of male company. This is the most frequent rationale for the deranged women in Romantic writing, and while the history of this myth may be difficult to delineate, its source is almost certainly the Hippocratic medical writings which recommended regular sexual intercourse (or pregnancy) as a cure for hysteria.[6] The long-standing belief in sexual abstinence as a prime cause of woman's disorder and derangement, stated as clearly in the medical writings of the Romantic period as in those of early Greece, lies at the heart of so many of our cultural assumptions about the nature and relations of woman and man. Some of the writings examined here are both consequence and cause of this peculiar but potent orthodoxy: they feed off the ideology they perpetuate.

The reasons for the predominance of the deranged woman in the mythology of Romantic and post-Romantic writings are not easily discovered. Certain coincidences may be helpfully adduced in order to suggest possibilities for a theoretical explanation: most notably a sharp increase in psychiatric writings in the second half of the eighteenth century; the symbolic liberation of lunacy from a method of treatment based on repression and restraint (seen most obviously in Pinel's famous gesture); or the professionalisation of psychiatric treatment. The history of 'Romantic' psychiatric medicine is indeed a very eventful one, but its surface features offer no obvious clues denoting reasons for literature's repeated exploitation of feminine derangement in the period. One signal ironic coincidence deserves particular attention. At the time of the birth of the therapeutic state,[7] art chooses not to represent its madwomen as subjects for therapy or rehabilitation, but (largely) as sufferers in the tragedy of 'natural' existence. It is the innate conservatism of artistic form that enforces its preference for presenting its madwomen in this way, and the emphasis therefore falls not on the ever-present potential for individual and social change, but on the fixed inevitability of a history that determines this tragic degeneration. An alternative explanatory theory for the madwoman's place in this mythology might begin by noting a vaguely ordered feminization of madness in the period: both the fear of the patient's violence and the violence used to repress were being purged out of contemporary accounts of the treatment of the insane, and subsequently lunacy and derangement attached themselves more readily to contemporary notions of femininity.

The strange patterns of behaviour attending the madwoman – the touching resonance of her gestures indicating the destruction of her former desires and their fragmentary afterlife – had particular attraction for the artists of an age of sensibility. Henry Mackenzie's man of feeling, Harley, finds his tour of Bedlam culminates in an encounter with a madwoman whose story is told by her keeper:

> She was beloved, if the story I have heard is true, by a young gentleman, her equal in birth though by no means her match in fortune: but Love, they say, is blind, and so she fancied him as

much as he did her. Her father, it seems, would not hear of their marriage, and threatened to turn her out of doors, if ever she saw him again. Upon this the young gentleman took a voyage to the West Indies, in hopes of bettering his fortune, and obtaining his mistress; but he was scarce landed, when he was seized with one of the fevers which are common in those islands, and died in a few days, lamented by every one that knew him. . . . The death of her lover had no effect on her inhuman parent; he was only the more earnest for her marriage with the man he had provided for her; and what between her despair at the death of the one, and her aversion to the other, the poor young lady was reduced to the condition you see her in.[8]

Following a series of male case details which fall easily into the routine of satiric *exempla* based on Augustan models (ruination by obsession with scientific theory, finance or scholarship), this meeting elicits not the implied presence of a moral lesson, but tears. There is a further distinction. In all cases the keeper plays the role of narrator, for madness rarely tells its own story, but here he offers neither anecdote nor fragment as formerly, but a complete story with a plot of cause and effect. As a result, the female lunatic has a text, to which her own utterances come as plaintive supplement:

'My Billy is no more!' said she, 'Do you weep for my Billy? Blessings on your tears! I would weep too, but my brain is dry; and it burns, it burns, it burns!' – She drew nearer to Harley. – 'Be comforted, young Lady,' said he, 'your Billy is in heaven.' 'Is he, indeed? and shall we meet again?'

Here suffering offers its own display for the sentimental voyeur, but while Harley regards the woman, he finds himself drawn into her drama. She sings to her audience, and siren-like, captivates it, proceeding then to identify Harley as bearing resemblance to her lost lover. The act of observation, dividing subject from object, has its economy broken down, and in its stead comes dialogue between sanity and insanity, the man of feeling and the woman deranged by feeling. In this dialogue differences become threatened, even blurred: Harley is and is not the lost lover; the woman retains a peculiar equanimity while Harley weeps, and she insists on departure while he clings to her hand irrationally. In addition, the madwoman believes Harley desires Billy's ring, and offers another plaited of gold thread taken from her clothing, a token therefore, of her lost life, commemorated in this new marriage.

It is a powerful moment in the novel and indeed, in the wider history of literature's madwomen, but the potential threat to the system of difference which sets male fortitude against female instability is only tentative. Within the emotive procedures and anticipated responses of the sentimental novel, the reader seemingly witnesses an instant of contact confusing in its effects, but behind this the scene is concerned to enact a far more potent and deeply engrained ritual wherein the woman is momentarily made whole again in the presence of the man. For Harley is effectively blessing the woman as he kisses her hand and receives her ring, and at that moment, her story is subjugated by his 'proper' response which encloses it within the history of the subject, the man of feeling. The episode's climax is therefore monopolised by Harley: the madwoman is confined not merely in her insanity, but also within his reactions, reinforced in his final reductive gesture of offering the keeper money. At this moment the madwoman is replaced in her original position as commodity, sold for the public's gaze, as indeed she was to be sold again to the readers of Mackenzie's novel, who purchased access to the promotion of feeling, the exercise of the truly warm and sympathetic sensibility.

If this is a likely *locus classicus* of the madwoman in the age of sensibility, then it has a rival for this position in Cowper's crazy Kate, who appears in Book 1 of *The Task*, 'The Sofa' (1785). Ample and obvious documentation for the attractions of this passage may be found in the attention given to it by artists such as Fuseli and Shepheard,[9] and in all likelihood it was responsible for the massive popularity enjoyed by poems depicting madwomen in the magazines and miscellanies of the 1790s.[10] The poem, sung 'for the fair' (line 7) is determined upon celebrating the virtues inherent in the natural world, as opposed to those of cultivated society. These latter include the sofa itself, which according to Cowper's fanciful history, is made in response to the discomforted murmerings of 'the softer sex' (line 71). 'The Sofa' is therefore addressed to women in the conventional mode of gallant satire, and it runs through a series of morally imbued scenes in the form of largely rural vignettes. The lines concerned with crazy Kate are distinct in that they provide a history. With precisely the same kind of detail to that offered by Mackenzie, Cowper's madwoman is provided with a story complete with a causal plot. While there are no other distinctive features that may persuade the reader to see in this passage more than the decorative pleasures of the imagination around which the whole text is structured, the fact that the poem is addressed to society's women suggests that it bears the scarcely concealed imprint of some dreadful satiric warning. At the same time, its easily assumed position in the series of vignettes allows it the disingenuous status of a sentimental tale:

> There often wanders one, whom better days
> Saw better clad, in cloak of satin trimmed
> With lace, and hat with splendid riband bound.
> A serving maid was she, and fell in love
> With one who left her, went to sea, and died.
> Her Fancy followed him through foaming waves
> To distant shores, and she would sit and weep
> At what a sailor suffers; Fancy too,
> Delusive most where warmest wishes are,
> Would oft anticipate his glad return,
> And dream of transports she was not to know.
> She heard the doleful tiding of his death –
> And never smiled again! and now she roams
> The dreary waste; there spends the livelong day,
> And there, unless when charity forbids,
> The livelong night. A tattered apron hides,
> Worn as a cloak, and hardly hides, a gown
> More tattered still; and both but ill conceal
> A bosom heaved with never ceasing sighs.
> She begs an idle pin of all she meets,
> And hoards them in her sleeve; but needful food,
> Though pressed with hunger oft, or comelier clothes,
> Though pinched with cold, asks never. – Kate is crazed.[11]

Here the madwoman is observed and no more. She is the

object of Cowper's inner eye, the active dominant principle to which the poem is constantly drawing attention as an imaginative *tour de force*. Subjected to this gaze, the woman's history is enclosed: she is allowed no voice and no active part in the drama. The play of signification is limited by the boundaries of a narrative intent on giving primacy to the act of looking, and the economy of subject and object is never threatened as it is in *The Man of Feeling*. The poignancy of the scene depends upon a subscription to the values it subtly asserts through alluding to the woman's lost life, the values of a defined social position, usefulness, the appreciation of charity, and above all, the presence of the man whose absence here is contiguous to fragmentation and loss of whole being.

These two important and enormously popular examples of early Romantic or sentimentalized madwomen bear archetypal relationships to the examples of derangement discussed in this study. At the same time, they embody the traces of important source material in their allusions to Shakespeare: Mackenzie's woman recalling Ophelia in her broken snatches of folk-song, while Cowper's follows an amalgam of patterns deriving from *King Lear*. In turn, these sources indicate and possibly determine important differences. Mackenzie's woman is confined. As an inmate of Bedlam she inhabits the eighteenth-century official realm of madness, symbolically reinforced by the famous tours which exhibited lunacy for the gratification of the sane. Cowper's Kate, however, moves in the feudalistic dimension of madness, wherein outcast lunacy wanders the wastes of the countryside. In historical terms these are large differences, for one passage relates an experience of madness which juxtaposes the privileges of the sane with the deprivations of the insane within the conditions of urban capitalism, while the other presents the sufferings of the insane through the analogue of the harsh rural landscape, wherein relief is only found through the unspoken law of unsolicited alms-giving. Given these distinctions it is remarkable how easily each passage collapses its individual history into an identical formula. Whatever the outer history of social and political events, the history of writing here asserts its own tyrannical conventions. This is an orthodoxy of writing woman's madness, concerned to naturalize it across massive differences by centralizing the absence of the man.

For the artists of the late eighteenth century, woman's madness is not mania, but derangement. It reorganizes the lost life of the past together with its promises and hopes for the future into a present obsessed by both, and unable in its suffering to distinguish between them. It articulates this suffering through a vocabulary of despair and loss, and it speaks therefore of disappointment and unfulfilled desire. Social deviance here rarely transforms itself into social revenge, and in this respect there is a sharp difference between this female stereotype and her predecessor, the witch. Yet simultaneously there is a similarity: the histories of witches and madwomen have shown them both to be subject to the same kind of diagnoses, and the same stigmatizing processes. These may be explained in terms of the moral responsibilities attached to women within what Foucault calls 'the politics of sex': 'the hysterization of women . . . was carried out in the name of the responsibility they owed to the health of their children, the solidity of the family institution, and the safeguarding of society.'[12] Neglect of these responsibilities during and after the eighteenth century, made the woman liable to a diagnosis that categorized her medically, whereas previously she may have been suspected as a source of *maleficium*. Witches traditionally caused illness in others: the madwoman, a social rather than theological deviant, embodies that illness in herself.

Following Cowper and Mackenzie, the late eighteenth century sustained its interest in madwomen largely through the 'original verses' of the magazines and Gothic novels and romances.[13] The existence of this material alerts us to the popularity of a motif, and for the most part, its handling shows little variation. Usually the present condition of madness or extreme melancholy is heightened by the recall of the past, indeed, the confusion of past and present may be the prime means of indicating derangement. The ballad mode is frequently employed, and in keeping with its conventions, the woman is given a voice so that her lament may be overheard. 'Ellen; or, the fair insane', published in *The Scots*

Plate 1: Johann Heinrich Füssli, *Mad Kate* (1806-7) oil on canvas, inv. nr. 1b-1955-7 (Freies Deutsches Hochstift Goethe-Museum, Frankfurt am Main). Photo: Ursula Edelman, Frankfurt am Main.

Plate 2: Henry Fuseli, *Woman with a Stiletto, Man's Head with a Startled Expression* (1810-20) (Ashmolean Museum, Oxford). Inscribed at top by an unknown hand 'Mary Anne' (Mary Anne Lamb).

Plate 3: Francis Danby, *Disappointed Love* (1821) oil (Victoria and Albert Museum, London). Reminiscent of Ophelia. 'Disappointed love' – a phrase much used in medical discourse to refer to the condition known as Erotomania.

Magazine in 1795, is a good example. The poem opens with Ellen's address to a stranger, as she enquires after her lost lover, and it then moves into a rehearsal of the imagined pleasures of meeting him again:

> Then we'll trip to yonder grove –
> There he told me first his love;
> And, when there, with kisses sweet,
> He'll the charming tale repeat!
>
> Fifty ways his fondness shew;
> Braid my locks, and bind my brow:
> Cull me flow'rs, or blithely play
> Many a pretty roundelay.
>
> See this chaplet! this he wove –
> Ah! how long delays my love!
> Know'st thou, stranger, where he strays?
> Can'st thou tell me why he stays?

Her lucid reliving of the past is a kind of reprieve from her madness, achieving a temporary sanity or phase of coherence dependent on the imagined presence of the man. The poem departs from the usual formula by including the detail of her desertation, her lover having committed suicide as a result of her infidelity:

> Pitiest thou my hapless lot? –
> Pity now availeth not!
> Envy's arts possess'd the youth,
> Ellen had betray'd his truth.
>
> Oh, I saw the deadly cup;
> Why should Bertram drink all up!
> None to leave me, was unkind –
> Yet, I would not stay behind.[14]

Accordingly, Ellen weakens, and 'wildly gazing', dies.

In line with the predominant moral attitudes of the day perhaps, her madness would be read as punitive, a just reward for her betrayal,[15] much as the woman's melancholy in 'The Penitent Mother' (published in the *Monthly Magazine and*

British Register, 1797) would have been seen as a proper consequence of her weakness. Here the mother weeps over her illegitimate child, and in the way of Wordsworth's mad mother, finds solace only in soothing her offspring ('Then hush, sweet babe! Thy cries give o'er,/Distract my tortur'd breast no more').[16] Not all the magazine poems work on an identical formula, however. 'Annabella' (written by the author of 'The Penitent Mother') employs the usual device of the overheard lament (again taking place over the child) and that of ending the poem with the woman's death in a state of madness or frenzy, but it establishes important topical references by presenting its subject as a war-widow, and as a consequence of this, the poem uses the 'ravings' of its protagonist as a form of protection for its powerful social condemnations:

> Oh! curs'd, thrice curs'd, be Glory's voice
> That thunders war and rage;
> That bids the soul of man rejoice
> To spare nor sex nor age!
>
> And thou, sweet babe! once all my joy,
> But now my greatest woe!
> Wilt thou the human race destroy,
> And earth with blood o'erflow?
>
> Oh! rather would this widow'd hand
> Cut short thy infant days,
> Then thou shouldst bid the fiend-like brand
> Of war and discord blaze![17]

Unlike 'Ellen; or, the fair insane', which is concerned to evoke the happiness of the past in the melancholy confusion of the present in order to imply a state of 'normal' womanhood, this poem uses insanity as a means of shifting the woman out of her required responses. Thus what were commonly thought of as maternal instincts (so important in poems like 'The Penitent Mother' or Wordsworth's 'Her Eyes are Wild') are defeated, and not by mere mania, but by the madness perceived by the woman in the rejoicing voice of glory. Whatever the technical achievements of its verse, the poem effects a neat reversal here in the sanity of its insane voice. It is this kind of potential, perhaps, that alerted Wordsworth to the possibilities of using the mad or deserted woman as a figure representative of the social injustices caused by war in the late eighteenth century.

Such possibilities almost find grounds for development in Southey's work of the 1790s, but the radical tendencies are not sustained in his use of closely related themes. 'Hannah' and 'The Ruined Cottage' from the *English Eclogues* (1799) both take as their theme declining, deserted or bereaved women, but neither poem extends its interest to embrace the issues presented in another of Southey's poems, 'The Complaints of the Poor' (1798) in which a lone woman with a child explains that she has to beg her way back to her parish because her husband serves as a soldier. Southey's popular poem of woman's madness, 'Mary, the Maid of the Inn' (reprinted at least eight times in the magazines),[18] turns its back on social concerns to exploit a different interest. Mary is driven mad not merely by being deserted, but by her traumatic recognition of her lover one stormy night in a ruined abbey as he is engaged in secreting a murdered corpse. Here madness is simply a means of exaggerating Gothic excess, and the madwoman is now a quaint, wild-eyed object in a fantastic romance. The Gothic novels of the period are also prone to use woman's derangement in this hyperbolic way. Sir Samuel Edgerton Brydges' *Mary de Clifford*, for example, concludes with the heroine's losing her mind in a delirious fever brought on by the news of her lover's death:

> she instantly fainted, and thence fell into fits, which were succeeded by a delirious fever, from whence she never sufficiently recovered to possess her intellects. For more than a week her life was not expected from hour to hour; at length the fever gradually subsided, and she seemed to grow much better. But the ramblings of her mind were exquisitely dreadful: she called on the name of Woodvile; she talked to him; she uttered such divine tenderness regarding him; she wrote such heavenly verses, yet so wild; that no persons who had the least touch sensibility, could bear to hear her without having their hearts almost broken. During this time her person, which generally wore the expression of an inspired melancholy, but was now and

then dressed up with a wild gaiety, was often more beautiful than before.[19]

It is perhaps in such texts as these that the insanity of the woman is building itself into an established convention or trope to be taken up by later writers. In the passage quoted, mania is the token of inexorable decay, and yet it transforms the subject into an untouchable icon. She becomes therefore the grand object of a tragic display. Caught in an aesthetic whose primary concern was to register the fine sensibility of human nature and promote appropriate responses from the reader, the woman's madness is the means of exaggerating the effects of loss and ultimately death, here extending itself back into the land of the living, as derangement clings to the hopes and promises of the conjoined life in a carefully orchestrated swan-song.

Notes

1. Michel Foucault, *Madness and Civilization. A History of Insanity in the Age of Reason*, translated by Richard Howard (London, 1971), pp. 6–7.
2. For a useful summary of archetypes and a discussion of their meanings, see Lillian Feder, *Madness in Literature* (Princeton, N.J., 1980), pp. 3–97.
3. Ibid., pp. 87–9.
4. Plato, *The Phaedo*, in *Plato's Dialogues*, translated by William Whewell (London, 1892), p. 128.
5. For a thorough historical survey, see Ilza Veith, *Hysteria: The History of a Disease* (Chicago and London, 1965).
6. Ibid., p. 11.
7. See Foucault (1971); and also Thomas S. Szasz, *The Manufacture of Madness* (London, 1971), a book which questions the remedial practices of the therapeutic state in a different way.
8. Henry Mackenzie, *The Man of Feeling*, edited by Brian Vickers (London, 1967), p. 33. All subsequent quotations and references are taken from this edition. Page numbers follow in parentheses.
9. Henry Fuseli, *Mad Kate* (1806–7). A reproduction of an aquatint from Shepheard's painting can be found in Max Byrd, *Visits to Bedlam: Madness and Literature in the Eighteenth Century* (Columbia, 1974).
10. See Robert Mayo, 'The Contemporaneity of the Lyrical Ballads', *PMLA*, 69 (1954), 486–52.

11. William Cowper, *The Task*, I, 534–56, *Cowper: Poetical Works*, edited by H. S. Milford (London, 1967).
12. Michel Foucault, *The History of Sexuality*, Vol. I, translated by Robert Hurley (London, 1979), pp. 146–7. Part of my commentary here derives from the arguments of Szaz (1971), who begins his book with an extended thesis on the historiography of witches and insanity.
13. Robert Mayo notes that bereaved and deserted women 'were almost a rage' in the 1790s and that the consequences commonly included madness. He lists some 39 poems about mad and deserted women (see Mayo, 1954). Gothic novels and romances featuring the same subjects in this period include the following: Sophia Lee, *The Recess, or, A Tale of other Times*, 3 vols (London, 1783–5), Clara Reeve, *The School for Widows*, 3 vols (London, 1791), Elisabeth Helme, *The Farmer of Inglewood Forest*, 4 vols (London, 1796), W. F. William, *Fitzmaurice*, 2 vols (London, 1800), J. H. Sarratt, *Koenigsmark, the Robber, or the Terror of Bohemia* (London, 1801), Mrs Isaacs, *Ariel, or, The Invisible Monitor*, 4 vols (London, 1801), Charlotte Dacre, *The Passions*, 4 vols (London, 1811).
14. *The Scots Magazine*, 57 (1795), 96.
15. See also 'The Penitent Prostitute', in *The Scots Magazine*, 50 (1788), 345–6.
16. *The Monthly Magazine and British Register*, 3 (1797), 142.
17. Ibid., 54.
18. See Mayo (1954). Southey's note to the poem states that its subject was made into a painting by 'Mr Barker' (possibly Barker of Bath), but I have not been able to trace this.
19. Sir Samuel Edgerton Brydes, *Mary de Clifford* (London, 1792).

CHAPTER TWO

Mad Women in Romantic Psychiatry

While woman's madness and derangement were being written into the literary texts of the Romantic period and beyond, it was receiving more detailed and direct treatment in the medical and psychiatric writings of the same period. Here may be found a huge volume of writings on nervous diseases, hysteria, derangement and insanity which rarely failed to discuss woman's vulnerability to mental and behavioural aberrations. If this body of discourse could be taken as a reservoir of its society's beliefs and practices, then we would be left in no doubt that it had a deeply established belief in the special proneness of woman to insanity, which went so far as to see it as a condition constantly attending her biological and social state. To take these works as ideological evidence (of whatever kind) is not the concern motivating this chapter, which will be presenting material not commonly available. Further, I wish to push my study towards the manner of writing insanity, towards an identification of the common means and rhetorical devices through which woman's derangement is established. After all, it is perhaps to be readily predicted that women are as likely to be distinguished within the diagnoses and definitions of madness as they are under any other patriarchal structure of belief, and to treat this body of writings as material for a thesis that has been proven time and time again – even though the political justice of such reiteration is unquestionable – would be beyond the brief this study has set itself. In conjunction with the work of this chapter, I have provided an appendix comprising case-studies taken from these and other contemporary works. Here

I am concerned first to summarize the common psychiatric ideas about woman's madness, and then to analyse them. The writers with whom I am concerned tend to concentrate their commentaries on certain conditions which they believe are peculiar in rendering woman vulnerable to derangement: her biological condition, her education or her social role, and her emotional sensitivity. While these are not the declared titles or heading of the writers themselves, they are sufficiently discernible as powerful and determining assumptions to be used here for the purposes of sub-division.

I

In *Outlines of Lectures on the Nature, Causes, and Treatment of Insanity*, Sir Alexander Morison cannot easily make up his mind whether women are more prone to insanity than men, and he concludes that this cannot be taken as an established fact.[1] Nevertheless, in arguing the question of statistical evidence, he has no apparent difficulty in conceiving that this could be the case:

> . . . it is generally understood that mental alientation is of more frequent occurence amongst females than amongst men. M. Esquirol says, that the number of insane males predominates over that of females in countries where the average temperature is either high or low. . . . In Great Britain and France however, he asserts that the number of insane females is greater; and this is the less extraordinary, because there exists in the female a variety of causes, as disorders of the menstrual function, pregnancy, parturition, and suckling; which are, of course, peculiar to sex.[2]

During menstruation, there is a vulnerability to a 'nervous state approaching hysteria', while childbearing 'seems to give to many women a predisposition to insanity'.[3] Sir William Ellis, writing a little earlier (1838), while not seeing the complexity of the woman's body as being a direct or unmitigated cause of insanity, notes that 'women who have any predisposition to insanity, seem, both during pregnancy and immediately after delivery, more susceptible of its attacks than at any other periods.' His explanation reveals the presence of the ancient theory of uterine displacement in his thinking, for Ellis asserts that 'after delivery, insanity more frequently arises from the brain sympathising with the uterus, from the stoppage of the lochia, or from its sympathising with the breasts, from cold, or from any other cause interrupting the secretion of the milk.'[4] This is not the Egyptian wandering womb of course, but the eighteenth-century theory of the nervous system's sympathetic concord, summarized neatly by Foucault, who adds a commentary on the privilege attributed to the woman's body in the theory:

> The entire female body is riddled by obscure but strangely direct paths of sympathy; it is always in an immediate complicity with itself, to the point of forming a kind of absolutely privileged site for the sympathies; from one extremity of its organic space to the other, it encloses a perpetual possiblity of hysteria.[5]

If the geography of the woman's body is charted by these complex interconnections, then the centralizing of the uterus within the sympathetic system creates a deterministic history which will identify monumental crises at the moments of childbirth, pregnancy and menstruation. Thus John Connolly, in *An Inquiry Concerning the Indications of Insanity*, writes:

> During pregnancy, partly perhaps from an undue circulation in the brain, and partly from a morbid state of the brain itself, explained by its sympathy with the states of the uterus, the mental faculties and moral feelings sometimes undergo similar modifications. Depraved sensations, great irritation, melancholy, the development of unusual propensities, as a propensity for stealing, or for saving or spending money, &C., are among the well-known accompaniments of the pregnant state: the variety depending, it would seem, on different portions of the brain being irritated in different cases.[6]

Connolly, shy of the word 'insanity' and preferring to talk about 'modifications of intellectual activity', also claims he has been witness to such aberrations manifest in a 'tendency to maniacal excitement . . . in cases of amenorrhea'.[7]

The chemistry of the brain and the uterus is indeed an

unstable one for the writers of this period, but it is not only married women who may suffer. Connolly's theories also show strong traces of the habitual suspicion accorded to the spinster's 'unnatural' condition. For the uterus of the unmarried woman, as well as that of the recently confined, 'is often the cause of mental disturbance of a most formidable aspect; and if the cause is overlooked, the patient will generally be treated unsuccessfully.'[8] This view of the peculiarly precarious nature of woman's sanity was shared by John Haslam, whose writings were accorded considerable respect around the turn of the century.[9] As medical officer at Bethlem (1795–1816), he had no doubt that womankind was at special risk. Menstruation might not be a cause of insanity, but it was frequently connected with the manifestation of its more extreme behavioural symptoms. Moreover, such cases were unlikely to resolve themselves in complete recovery.[10] Working from Bethlem's statistics, Haslam claimed a greater preponderance of insanity in women than in men, and he explained this by reference to the familiar 'natural processes which women undergo'.[11]

Thomas Arnold's *Observations of the Nature, Kinds, and Causes and Prevention of Insanity* (second edition, 1806) sees insanity as deriving from a number of causes including 'change produced in the animal system in consequence of lying-in, suppression of the menses' amongst others, and these may be so violent as to lead to suicide.[12] Later in his work, Arnold elaborates on the vulnerability of the woman's body to malfunctions of this kind which may lead to insanity, developing a theory that asserts the even flow of blood as a means to the preservation of a stable constitution: when blood does not find its necessary egress, it may flood the brain, or cause the brain to suffer from the violent agitation induced in the heart and arteries.[13] For Arnold, the woman's mind is forever susceptible to the potential instability of her body. That instability is so pervasive as to reverse the expected norms of sanity and insanity:

. . . we cannot but admire the kind superintendence of Providence, and the surprising efficacy of Nature, in the preservation of lying-in women; and ought rather to wonder that they so often escape, than that they sometimes suffer, violent disorders after delivery, and that delirium, and insanity, are not the least frequent of these disorders.[14]

Here nature surprises by a wondrous operation working against the odds she herself has created for woman. Madness is staved off by God and nature, even while it pursues the woman relentlessly in the very complexity of her biology.

Nineteenth-century psychiatric care is characterized in terms of its management of the patient as opposed to the exercise of restraint. The 'moral managers', as they have been called,[15] sought the primary causes of madness in life-style, and consequently placed great emphasis on regimen, conduct and expectations. Often reacting to the common notion that insanity in Britain occurred with greater frequency than elsewhere, and was also increasing, this school of thought and practice habitually turned its gaze on custom and education, and within this field of vision it located the woman as a *prima facie* example of the abused constitution. While man's robustness protected him to some extent from the injuries of a decadent society, woman's frailty made her a permanently liable victim.

Thomas Trotter's *A View of the Nervous Temperament* (1807), so convinced of woman's vulnerability, begins with a demographic medical classification of the urban population which has as its final class 'the female sex, consisting of the higher, middling and lower orders of women'. Whereas differences of status and occupation apply to men, woman's experience is so homogeneous across the classes as to preclude the question of real differences. For Trotter, 'the diseases of which we now treat, are in a manner the inheritance of the fair sex: when to these we superadd all the preposterous customs of fashionable life, need we wonder at the numerous instances of bad health and feeble existence, so often to be met with among them.'[16] In a manner which recalls the misogynistic satire of the eighteenth century which was concerned to distil the ills of fashionable society into the frame of the woman, Trotter's treatise transforms the metaphoric into the literal by representing the nervous illnesses of women as the indicators of social debility. Thus he identifies some familiar targets: stays and lacing, tea-drinking ('particularly hurtful to women') and novel-reading ('to the female mind in particular . . . this species of iterary poison has been often fatal').[17] But for Trotter, women are not merely scapegoats embodying social decadence. It is not only that their illness is society's illness, for the terms are often reversed in his writing, so that society's illness is the illness of women themselves, and they spread it like some dreadful contagion. His text comes from Deuteronomy, 28.56, ('The tender and delicate woman among you, which would not adventure to set the sole of her foot upon the ground for delicateness and tenderness her eye shall be evil toward the husband of her bosom, and toward her son, and toward her daughter') which he extends in such a way as to render women permanently responsible in the act of giving birth: 'From having injured her own frame by refinements in living, the mother thus sows the seeds of disease in the constitutions of her children: hence a weak body, delicate nerves, and their consequence, a sickly existence, become hereditary.'[18] Women are not merely ill, they are in themselves an insidious disease sapping the strength of traditional masculine virtue. Wealth and luxury are undermining social norms but it is the 'feminizing' of custom and habit, Trotter complains, that represents the greater threat through 'the general effeminancy of manners, that is rapidly consuming the manly spirit and physical strength of this age.'[19]

What Trotter takes to be distinctly female traits and habits become the preconditions of nervous debilities, including insanity. Great stress is placed on strength and exercise, from which he believes the women of his society are kept by what he takes to be their pampered existence and misinformed education. Thus giving birth is extremely dangerous in the contemporary world, whereas under the conditions of 'bountiful nature, unfettered in her operations . . . the robust rustic . . . attends her husband in the field in a few days'. Modern education, he suggests, 'refines on this tenderness of frame'.[20]

The nervous conditions about which Trotter writes are described in such a way as to make them constantly contiguous to his characterization of women: the source of these conditions is located in the over-refinements of modern life, archetypally inscribed in the stereotype of the fashionable woman which he so frequently draws upon; their perpetration rests with the 'effeminacy of manners' and the excessive tenderness of the female constitution. A similar conflation of traditional misogynistic feminine metaphors with descriptions of the conditions attending insanity occurs in the work of John Connolly. Attempting to distinguish between what he calls 'true insanity' and other unstable conditions, Connolly describes an area between madness and normality that is inhabited by the characteristics of volatility and inconstancy:

> Such individuals are a constant source of uneasiness. . . . They are zealous friends, or even indiscreet, but not capable of steady attachment: and they are revengeful and unscrupulous in their animosities. This inconstancy of character may play within an extensive range without insanity; but the separate actions, by which it is evinced, approach to what is irrational; and the wavering and inconstant mind itself is certainly allied to that which is insane. In its slightest form, and that which is the least possible deviation from the sound mind, it has often been described as the female character, 'varium et mutabile semper;'
> 'And variable as the shade,
> By the light quivering aspen made;'
> and the minds of some women present the most striking illustrations of it. Yet it is not peculiar to the sex.[21]

Despite the disclaimer, Connolly makes his point by a forcible reference to a mythology of womankind reinforced by literature and other writings. Here 'the female character' is a step – however slight – along the road to madness, 'allied to that which is insane'. A proximity of a similar kind is insisted on by John Barlow in *On Man's Power over himself to prevent or control Insanity* (1849). Barlow does not characterize madness itself through femininity, for his emphasis on moral management leads him to present woman not as naturally weak, but strong, and only defiled by custom into feebleness. Therefore woman stands as a victim of social perversion, not as its source. Indeed, Barlow argues that woman's real destination lies in her role as the 'high-minded purifier of society' since physiologists have demonstrated that the 'organs of thought are proportionally larger in woman than in man: and many a bright example has shewn how well they *can* be employed.'[22] Such is society's mismanagement, however, that women are far more frequently mad than men. It is, argues Barlow, 'a plain statistical fact' that there are nearly a third more women than men in lunatic asylums, and this derives from educational practice which teaches not self-government, decisiveness and independence, but mute obedience. Women suffer more than men from this because the life they enjoy after their formal education is insufficiently distinguished from it:

> But if this be the case as regards the male sex, how much more fearfully then is it of the female! Here the Drawing-room but perpetuates the inertias of the Nursery, – and woman, so largely endowed by nature, is degraded by social prejudice, and the frivolous education consequent on it, till she is left at the mercy of events, the creature of impulse and of instinct.[23]

Much the same ground is occupied by George Man Burrows, who, unlike Barlow, believes that more men than women are confined in asylums. He is concerned to put this down to drunkenness 'which prevails most among males', and this he believes to be sufficiently widespread to overturn the more likely imbalance of women to men deriving from feminine vulnerability:

> Many circumstances in the physical and moral condition of women, from the epoch of puberty to the critical period, would lead us to conclude that more women than men become insane in every country and every place. . . . Women are certainly exposed to more natural causes of physical excitation and irritation than men. Besides menstruation, parturition and all its consequences, women also, from education or occupation, are more obnoxious to superstitious and fanatical impressions.[24]

Elsewhere in his writings Burrows expands on this susceptibility, arguing that the introduction of new religious enthusiasms can be a particularly potent catalyst provoking insanity in women. After citing six case studies he remarks:

It will scarcely escape remark, that five out of the six examples cited are females. The selection is not designed. Were every similar case recorded, I believe nearly the same disproportion would be found between the sexes: at least, such is my experience. There are doubtless, physical causes in the female economy, whence women are more prone to insanity than men; but the moral causes superinducing it are still more numerous. Physically, man is more robust, and has less sensibility, or as the physiologist would have it, irritability, than woman; morally, his education is more solid, and his pursuits more active and definite. The education of females is generally showy, rather than substantial, and as they naturally possess more ardent and susceptible minds, want of active occupation becomes a most dangerous enemy to them. Thus circumstanced, if any object present itself sufficiently striking, they are apt to embrace it without due examination; and if of a nature to excite, it soon exercises an inordinate influence. Nothing is so conducive to this effect as new views of religion . . .[25]

Within the considerable body of writing concerned to stress the moral management of insanity (of which only a small proportion is represented here),[26] women assume a special place. They are constantly being evoked as examples of educational malpractice, or of feeblemindedness compounded by physical weakness, and as a result they are consistently subject to a process of marginalization that tends to equate their occupation and status with an abnormal condition. Indeed, so deeply implicated are they in these writings with the description of nervous debility and derangement, if not always with insanity itself, that feminity and mental illness come very close to being in a relation of mutual definition.

A similar equation may be found in the writings which identify emotional trauma as an agent inducing madness. Given literature's fondness for explaining woman's derangement similarly, these theories are probably the most consequential for this study. There is very little evidence, however, to suggest that writers of the period with which we are dealing saw emotional disturbance as the sole cause of insanity, thereby conceptualizing it as a disease of the mind only. Rather, they supposed that the emotional dramas with which they were concerned had immediate and important physical repercussions, and that these, in turn, either through nervous sympathy or a similarly conceptualized map of the body's geogrpahy, affected the brain.

It is perhaps not surprising that in an age of sensibility Erasmus Darwin saw sensibility itself as a metaphor through which a complex theory of the connections between mind and body could be articulated. For Darwin, the 'irritable' constitution is that with the most vital network of nervous connections. The least irritable constitutions are those of low nervous conductivity, wherein 'blockages' manifest themselves physically. Excessive conductivity, however, has an adverse effect upon the mind. Thus it is the constitution of developed 'sensibility' which is most prone to insanity: 'the constitutions most liable to convulsions are those which most readily become torpid in some part of the system, that is, which possess less irritability; and that those most liable to insanity, are such as have excess of sensibility.'[27] Darwin is concerned to classify types of insanity, and he lists one of particular significance – 'Erotomania (or) Sentimental love'. This is a species of madness to which he believes women are vulnerable, for unlike men who have 'not had leisure to cultivate their taste for visible objects, and have not read the works of poets and romance-writers', they are educated 'with an idea of being chosen' and not of choosing. The fantasies and desires thus engendered, Darwin implies, can be dangerous.[28]

David Hartley also subscribed to the sympathetic notion of the nervous system and claimed that the causes of madness were both physical and mental, either acting as the primary cause: 'the bodily cause lays hold of that passion or affection, which is most disproportionate; and the mental cause, when that is primary, generally waits till some bodily distemper gives it full scope to exert itself.'[29] It is the passions that are highlighted in Hartley's discussion of madness, and while he does not treat of woman's insanity as a separable or distinct case, his description of the individual conditions under which insanity is likely to evolve accords closely to contemporary commonplaces about womankind. He distinguishes between madness and melancholy, but he regards both as conditions similar in kind. Melancholy may be caused by 'too much application of the mind, especially to the same objects and ideas, violent and long-continued passions'. It leads to 'absurd desires, hopes, and fears' which must be resisted to maintain sanity, for if the sufferer becomes 'permanently persuaded of the reality of very groundless hopes and fears' he or she proceeds to madness. For Hartley, passion itself is a kind of madness, albeit temporary, and moreover 'violent fits of passion, and frequent recurrences of them, must, from the nature of the body, often transport persons, so that they shall not be able to recover themselves, but fall within the limits of the distemper called madness emphatically.'[30]

Broadly accepting the views of writers such as Hartley and Darwin, and arguing that insanity derives from a 'diseased action in the brain', Sir W. C. Ellis thought women particularly susceptible because of their strong emotions of grief. This he saw as a very likely cause of madness, and within this category of the insane, 'females form by far the largest proportion'.[31] Most, he suggests, are deranged by the loss of children, but he also notes disappointment in love and jealousy – offering case-studies of women as examples – as emotional disturbances from which madness may develop.

Thomas Trotter is in agreement with Ellis, while being less dramatic in limiting the effects of emotional disturbances to the vague area of nervous illness. He takes grief as the most traumatic emotion, believing the 'attachment of a mother to the infant . . . the strongest of all human passions'. The death of a child, accordingly, could denude the mother of the power of reason:

> In some instances of maternal affliction, we have observed the faculties so powerfully oppressed by sorrow; so absorbed in the contemplation of one object, that the mind appeared almost, or wholly unconscious of its own existence, and scarcely attended to a single external impression. In such cases the intervals of reason, or consciousness, were only to be marked by sighs, groans, and tears, as the expression of grief.[32]

After the mother's bereavement, Trotter believes 'disappointed love' to be the most common factor in woman's nervous illness. Again the woman is represented as feeble and passive in opposition to man's energy and activity. Further, the woman's liability is increased by a propensity to conceal her emotions:

> Next to these heart-rending emotions of parental sorrow, may be reckoned the effects of disappointed love, on the sensible female frame. In the male sex the active pursuits of business or pleasure, more quickly supplant tender impressions; and men much sooner regain that mental tranquility which fits them for the busy scenes of life. This is not the case with the fair sex; for the influence on both body and mind, seems to be in proportion to the concealed struggle of attachment. The heart obtains relief in pouring forth its complaint, and acquires resolution when this is done: but the hidden passion burns the fiercer by being suppressed. The separation of the parties, and long engagements that procrastinate marriage, are often fatal to health.[33]

Morison believed sustained grief could lead to madness, and was a frequent cause of insanity in women. Erotomania, wherein the 'suffererer is generally a female', revealed itself in restlessness, melancholy and silence, the only expression of grief being found by the subject 'continually writing the name of the beloved object on paper, on the walls of the room, or on the ground'.[34] Under the category of 'bashful insanity', Thomas Arnold also identified concealed desire as a cause of woman's madness: 'bashfulness is sometimes a striking symptom, where the insanity is owing to concealed love: and seems to be on very uncommon, or unnatural prelude to that dreadful kind of insanity the *furor uterinus*.'[35]

The hysterical woman, besieged from within by her suppressed desire, is a figure frequently evoked in Robert Brudenell Carter's work on hysteria. Carter has no doubt about the powerful effects of emotional traumas, and in common with most medical writers of his time, he believes they instigate biological disorders which in turn induce behavioural aberrations. He proposes 'that these derangements are much more common in the female than in the male – women not only being prone to the emotions, but also more frequently under the necessity of endeavouring to conceal them.'[36] The most violent feeling from which hysteria derives, he argues, is 'sexual passion'.[37] While he refutes physical disorders as a primary agent of derangement, he

regards them as contributory elements in that they may
provoke emotions and desires. Thus he disregards
malfunction of the uterus as an origin of hysteria, but such
complaints as menstrual difficulties may be of relevance if
they succeed in promoting thoughts of a sexual nature.[38]

Carter believes that regular but not excessive sexual
intercourse is a prerequisite of a stable mental constitution.
Woman's emotional range is larger than man's 'partly from
that natural conformation which causes the former to feel,
under circumstances where the latter thinks', but also
because social conventions demand that women conceal their
feelings. The act of repression encourages the growth of
emotion and desire, and ultimately this leads to derangement.
Woman's sexuality compounds the problem, for Carter
believes female desire to be particularly strong: 'it will add
immensely to the forces bearing upon the female, who is often
much under its dominion; and who, if unmarried and chaste,
is compelled to restrain every manifestation of its sway.' Man,
however, 'having such facilities for its gratification' is
practically immune from hysterical attacks, but Carter claims
that in recorded cases of male hysteria the sufferers have often
been found continent, 'a circumstance which may have
assimilated the effects of amativeness upon them to those
which are constantly witnessed in the female'.[39] It is not
surprising, therefore, to find that Carter's deranged women
are often located in identical circumstances to that common
literary stereotype, the deserted woman. Women of strong
passions separated from their husbands, he asserts, are
especially vulnerable.[40]

Carter's affirmation of sexual desire and frustration as a
source of feminine derangement takes its place happily in the
mythical tradition which sees the woman as sexually
complex, mysterious, and simultaneously dependent on the
man for gratification, and thereby, for mental stability.
Darwin's ideas of the inherent dangers of a 'torpid system'
also imply the necessity of the maintaining regular exercise in
all 'animal' functions.[41] Thomas Arnold, while believing that
'excessive venery enervates the body and debilitates the
mind',[42] also recommended regular sexual intercourse as a
means of preserving mental health. Frustration could cause

'appetitive insanity' (satyriasis in men and nymphomania in women) and while these are not very common, women are more likely to suffer than men. The reasons, Arnold suggests, are obvious – 'the delicacy, timidity, restraint, and peculiar natural economy, of the fair sex, rendering them more liable to the one; than the licentious freedom of indulgence, in which men too generously allow themselves, leaves them in danger of the other.' In the prevention of insanity, the 'venereal appetite' should be 'used with so much moderation as, not to debilitate, but to animate, and strengthen, both the body, and the mind.'[43]

II

In the manufacture of nineteenth-century madness, women are an essential element. Not only do they provide vocabulary by which insanity and derangement may be articulated (through the fund of terms growing around 'effeminacy' and related concepts) they also provide the prime sites wherein new and old theories can be promulgated and tested: theories of complex nervous networks, emotional sensitivity, and educational practice or self-regulation. These are the areas in which late eighteenth and early nineteenth-century medicine develops an aetiology of madness and a therapeutic policy, and in each case its crucial arguments and exemplifications are able to cluster happily around the figure of the woman. This figure, of course, derives not from clinical observation or 'field-study' for it is not empirical in its derivation but mythological or literary.

Foucault has argued that one of the most significant changes that madness undergoes in the eighteenth century is in the way that it enters into a new and oppositional relationship with sanity. As derangement became less and less the sign of contact with higher truth found on another plain of existence, or that found in divine inspiration, so it became secularized and assigned to a definite social space, the place of confinement, the position of exclusion. Confinement has a special meaning for Foucault, in that here madness 'ceased to be the sign of another world' becoming instead 'the paradoxical manifestation of non-being' and in an important sense therefore, 'madness is immediately perceived as difference'.[44]

In the writings presented as samples here, which represent a small selective study of the material available, woman's madness offers itself as a particularly definite form of difference. Woman's difference, the otherness to man never translated to otherness itself, or *her* otherness, is confirmed and compounded by the otherness, the difference, of insanity.[45] Within the kind of model Foucault proposes, this process of mutual confirmation can be seen to work in the opposite direction, that is, from insanity to woman. Insanity, now seeking to define itself against what is, rather than locating itself in another world, ranges across the field of social being and distinguishes itself by a regular series of associations with the distinct signs of difference, indications of antitheses to the natural, the normal, the social. In this search it repeatedly encounters woman, not – so to speak – as a social or cultural reality, a living subject, but as a signifier, a conveniently aggregated indicator which in the very act of pointing away from normality, also points back towards it to denote the direction of deviation. In this sense woman and madness share the same territory. To use another figure, they may be said to enter a concentric relationship around a central point occupied by a fundamentally male normality. Like some insidious virus, insanity therefore invades the mythology of woman, finding therein a semiotic fund that it may use for the purposes of self-definition. And part of this fund comes pat, almost ready-made, in the conveniently presented package of hysterical affliction, a permanent attachment to the figure of the woman, and now available for co-option by the new, secularized insanity though the important precedent that hysteria, too, could be seen as a disease of the mind.[46] Although this had been established quite early, at the end of the seventeenth century, the secularizing of the institutional network of insanity took much longer, and thus while woman's hysteria could be put down to the weakness of her mind combining with her bodily complexity throughout the eighteenth century, insanity discovered a very similar nexus or equation somewhat later, at which point, therefore, it was able to enclose the same mythology.

The history of psychiatric care and practice in the eighteenth and nineteenth centuries bears all the outward marks of a science developing through empirical method. Observation of the patient (including post-mortem examinations of the brain) performs a prime role, with many of the major writers on insanity being in positions of authority in the asylums themselves; development of devices for therapy and cure are plentiful; restraint and punitive confinement are abandoned in the declarations of philanthropic conscience and desire for rehabilitation; psychiatric professionalization becomes fully developed; finally, the era closes with Freud and Breuer developing new therapeutic methods for the treatment of hysteria which will lead to the 'great truth' of psychoanalysis, with its massive relevance for the definition of normality. But even while the steady gradient of general social improvement might seem to indicate the upward path of scientific truth, apparently confirmed in out own century by the testimony of technology, the writing of women's madness in the nineteenth century refuses to endorse the notion of historical development to which our culture is wedded. This writing takes place in the arena of Romantic medicine, which although officially recognized as running through a distinctly European or German line from Schelling to Freud,[47] may also be witnessed here in the Romantic insistence on the search for origins, the fixing of a natural state that is subsequently corrupted, the stressing of a new concept of education through the acknowledgement of individualism, and the identification of the transforming powers of the emotions, the capacity to feel and suffer within the tragic permanence of the great passions.

This Romanticism, in common with other kinds, presents its critique of the way things are by reference to the way things originally were, within a mythology of its own devising. This mythology is replete with values of usefulness, fortitude, industry, self-control, propagation of the species, proper regimen governing the complexities of the body; and in the centralizing of these positives, women are consistently serving as negative exemplifications, corruptions of original states. Thus while the work of those recommending moral management seemingly proposes a way out of the deterministic deadlock of the physiologists who placed women permanently at the mercy of their complex biology, they may only do so by deriding and relegating what they choose to see as the current occupational condition of women in their society. And in depicting what they see as the contemporary state of things, they do not provide access to the real, a historical actuality, for they are clearly reproducing conventional tropes through which the mythology of women has evolved: women read pernicious novels, they drink pernicious tea, are full of sick fantasies, their feeble bodies denote feeble minds, they are inconstant, impetuous, and above all, in need of male moral management, which may lead them some way towards a recognition of the natural and original masculine conditions, here often represented by the 'robust rustic'. In all these writings men are represented as more successful in the art of self-government than women, and that, of course, is a very old story.

If man is the implied absence in the writings of moral management and educational therapy, then the absence of man is an even larger void in those theories concentrating on emotional trauma and its relationship with the chemistry of the body. Here the presence of the man, and more specifically, the phallus, is a consistently suggested remedy for derangement. The continent woman is likely to suffer physical and emotional effects. She may have menstrual or uterine difficulties which subsequently disturb the brain. Alternatively or in addition, her unrequited desire is a sufficiently powerful emotion to produce a similar effect. Again, the figure of the woman projected is a figure of incompleteness. She is a creature of partial being, lacking wholeness, and most significantly, of secret, concealed and probably excessive desire. In this way, the desire of the woman for the man is given as an unnatural quality, for it is uncertain of its proper measurement and claims, dwelling in the clandestine and alien region of the imagination. Just as literature (as I shall later show) frequently seeks to locate and expose this secret life, to explode the fantastic nature of woman's desire, so medical discourse seeks to register the profound disquiet and suspicion it harbours for the same phenomenon. It implies a great moral difference between desire and need: woman's desire has no self-knowledge and clings to the impossible, as in its excessive grief for the dead, whereas woman's needs are self-evidently described in her biological function as man's sexual partner and the bearer of children.

Yet most remarkably of all, even in what one might suppose to be Romanticism's safest and sanest haven for women, the period of childbirth and nursing, insanity makes one of its largest claims. Anthropologists might point out that this association has its counterpart in those societies in which women giving birth are taboo, and no doubt the presence of madness here may be partially understood as performing an ostracizing act proceeding from an immense anxiety about the powerful and mysterious body which not only brings forth life but also sustains it. Inside this framework, however, we may be witnessing something else, the pathologizing of woman herself in the act which most characterizes her difference. These writers choose to make no real discrimination, in terms of the effects they cause, between childbirth and menstruation: both are natural, yet natural causes of pathological conditions which are thus inextricably secured to the natural state of womankind.[48] Women, therefore, are naturally ill. The categorization of insanity chooses not only to isolate them within its genera, but to shape certain of those genera by way of the woman's character and functions, making these inseparable from the disease itself.

Notes

1. Sir Alexander Morison, M.D., *Outlines of Lectures on the Nature, Causes, and Treatment of Insanity*, edited by T. C. Morison (London, 1848), p. 289.
2. Ibid., p. 288.
3. Ibid., p. 289, p. 281.
4. Sir W. C. Ellis, M.D., *A Treatise on the Nature, Symptoms, Causes and Treatment of Insanity* (London, 1838), p. 89, pp. 90–1.

5. Michel Foucault, *Madness and Civilization. A History of Insanity in the Age of Reason*, translated by Richard Howard (London, 1971), pp. 153–4. An important source of this body of thinking lies in the works of William Harvey, who had argued that 'the uterus is a most important organ and brings the whole body to sympathise with it.' As a consequence, women who remain unmarried 'are seized with serious symptoms – hysterics, furor unterinus, &C. or fall into a cathectic state, and distemperatures of all kinds. All animals, indeed, grow savage when in heat, and unless they are suffered to enjoy one another, become changed in disposition. In like manner women occasionally become insane through ungratified desire.' See Richard Hunter and Ida Macalpine, *Three Hundred Years of Psychiatry, 1535–1860* (London, 1963).

6. John Connolly M.D., *An Inquiry Concerning the Indications of Insanity* (London, 1830), p. 234.

7. Ibid., p. 239.

8. Ibid., p. 258. See also David Hartley, *Observations on Man, his Frame, his Duty and his Expectations*, 2 vols (London, 1791). Hartley maps the sympathetic connections of the body more precisely, suggesting that there are two prime sites for the origins of insanity, those of the body and the mind: 'the bodily cause lays hold of that passion or affection, which is most disproportionate: the mental cause, when that is primary, generally waits till some bodily distemper gives it full scope to exert itself' (I, 400–1). In the case of women, 'the uneasy states of the *uterus* are propagated to the brain, both immediately, i.e. by first affecting the stomach, and thence the brain' (I, 399).

9. John Haslam, *Observations on Insanity, 1798, superseded by Observations on Madness and Melancholy: including Practical Remarks on those Diseases; together with Cases: and an Account of the Morbid Appearances on Dissection*, second edition (London, 1809). For an account of Haslam's career and other writings, see Hunter and Macalpine (1963).

10. Haslam (1809): 'Insanity and epilepsy are often connected with menstruation, and suffer an exacerbation of their proxysms at the period when this discharge happens, or ought to take place' (p. 215).

11. Ibid., 'The natural processes, which women undergo, of menstruation, parturition, and of preparing nutriment for their infant, together with the diseases, to which they are subject at these periods, and which are frequently remote causes of insanity, may, perhaps, serve to explain their greater disposition to this malady' (pp. 245–6).

12. Thomas Arnold, *Observations on the Nature, Kinds, Causes and Prevention, of Insanity*, second edition, 2 vols (London, 1806), I, 187–8.

13. Ibid., II, 144–5.

14. Ibid., II, 146.

15. For a full documentary history, see Vieda Skultans, *Madness and Morals* (London, 1975).

16. Thomas Trotter, *A View of the Nervous Temperament*, second edition

(London, 1807), p. 37, p. 52.

17. Ibid., pp. 72–4, 80–1, 90.
18. Ibid., p. 53.
19. Ibid., pp. 155–6.
20. Ibid., pp. 36, 50.
21. Connolly (1830), pp. 174–5.
22. John Barlow, *On Man's Power over himself to prevent or control Insanity* (London, 1849), pp. 43, 44.
23. Ibid., pp. 43, 44.
24. George Man Burrows, *Commentaries on the Causes, Forms, Symptoms and Treatment, Moral and Medical, of Insanity* (London, 1828), pp. 239–40, 243.
25. George Man Burrows, *An Inquiry into Certain Errors relative to Insanity; and their Consequences; Physical, Moral and Civil* (London, 1820), pp. 215–6.
26. For further reading and a bibliographical guide, see Skultans (1975), and Hunter and Macalpine (1963).
27. Erasmus Darwin, M.D., *Zoonomia; or, the Laws of Organic Life*, 2 vols (London,1 794), II, 354.
28. Ibid., II, 363–4. Darwin goes on to cite literary examples.
29. Hartley (1791). See note 8.
30. Ibid., I, 399–400.
31. Ellis (1838), p. 71.
32. Trotter (1807), pp. 85–6.
33. Ibid., p. 87.
34. Morison (1848), pp. 117, 206.
35. Arnold (1806), I, 187–8.
36. Robert Brudenell Carter, *On the Pathology and Treatment of Hysteria* (London, 1853), pp. 25–6.
37. Ibid., pp. 29–30.
38. Ibid., p. 36.
39. Ibid., p. 33.
40. Ibid., p. 35.
41. Darwin (1794), II, 354. See also the passage on 'amatorial copulation', I, 456.
42. Arnold (1806), II, 82.
43. Ibid., II, 143, II, 325.
44. Foucault (1971), pp. 115–6.
45. See Shoshana Felman, 'Women and Madness: The Critical Phallacy', *Diacritics* (1975), 5, No. 4, 2–10, and particularly pp. 3–4, where the author explains Irigaray's feminism in the Derridean terms of the distinction between the woman as opposite and different: 'Theoretically subordinated to the concept of masculinity, the woman is viewed by the man as *his* opposite, that is to say, as *his* other, the negative of the positive, and not, in her own right, different, other, Otherness itself.' Simone de Beauvoir's thinking is also in evidence here.
46. Ilza Veith, *Hysteria: The History of a Disease* (Chicago and London,

1970) traces this back to the work of Thomas Sydenham whose work on hysteria in the late seventeenth century was the first to include the disease as an affliction of the mind. See pp. 140–4.

47. See George M. Rosen, 'Romantic Medicine: A Problem in Historical Periodization', *Bulletin of the History of Medicine*, 25 (1951), 149–58, and particularly p. 151. Vieda Skultans (1975) categorizes the moral managers and the debate surrounding their methods under the title 'psychiatric Romanticism'.

48. For a fuller account of this body of writings and its history see Vieda Skultans, *English Madness: Ideas on Insanity*, 1580–1890 (London, 1979). Chapter VI, 'Feminity and Illness' traces the pathologizing of woman's condition.

CHAPTER THREE

Bereavement, Desertion and Decay:

Wordsworth's deranged women and the fractured family

We have been taught to read Wordsworth in a number of ways, but principally as the poet of the human heart. His high reputation is asserted in commentaries upon his sympathies, his ability to provide correlatives of emotional conditions in delicately contrived poetic formulae, and of course his philosophical sagacity. In fact he has been accepted on his own terms, for the critical estimation relies on a narrative which derives from the *Preface to the Lyrical Ballads*. It recounts how Wordsworth set out to recover areas of experience believed lost to the poetic tradition he inherited, and how his texts provide access to humanistic truth, received in affective readings. It notes his high moral concern with the poet's responsibility to changing social conditions, and it documents his struggles with language and the problems of writing for a readership expanding across class barriers.

It is as well to return to Wordsworth's own commentary on some of these issues. What he and many of his critics rely upon is a trust in universalism, a dependence on the permanence of passions, articulated in a language and style that invite emotional participation: the object of poetry is 'truth, not individual and local, but general, and operative; not standing upon external testimony, but carried alive into the heart by passion'. As a consequence Wordsworth has no use for the mannered diction of coterie art. He wants a new bourgeois language of common sense, a language of prose, and the erasure of distinctions receives its endorsement through the 'natural' metaphor of the body:

the bodies in which both of them are clothed may be said to be of the same substance, their affections are kindred, and almost identical, not necessarily differing even in degree; Poetry sheds no tears 'such as Angels weep', but natural and human tears; she can boast of no celestial ichor that distinguishes her vital juices from those of prose; the same human blood circulates through the veins of them both.[1]

This universalism, which will admit of differences of degree (where appropriate) but not of kind is characteristic of the philosophy which is the effective *raison d'être* for Wordsworth's poetry, the philosophy that will hold all experience in common, but particularly emotional experience. Thus our emotional lives are played out on the same plane, even though the range of events which govern these lives may be small, and the range of emotions only moderate, the supposition is that we could all feel what others feel, and that poetry aspires to reproduce the emotions of others in the reader.

While this Romantic notion became the reason why poetry was taught in schools in our own century and an essential part of the valuation of poetry in the universities, in Wordsworth's day it formed the keystone of his commitment to the role of poetry in what he saw as a democratized culture. He believed that all could understand what others felt, or at least realize the significance of these feelings, regardless of divisions of class or gender. The man's experience is therefore the woman's, the rustic peasant's experience is also that of the urban reader's. This is the assumption upon which Wordsworth proceeded in his early years as a poet. It is denial of difference; an assumption which requests of the reader full moral responsibility in exchange for the tears she or she sheds; an assumption which also governed the philanthropical movements of the late eighteenth century.

No doubt those movements provided relief for some of those suffering at the sharp end of a rapidly developing capitalist economy, but most historians would agree that they are an essential part of the bourgeois world which gave that economy its full support. Likewise, it would be a mistake, on the basis of the recognition of good intentions, to see the individualism of Wordsworth's poetry as being divorced from the world which produced it, to see it, in other words, as his own particular and inspired insight into what many critics would still regard as truth. It is particularly difficult to resist the systems of thinking promulgated by Wordsworth himself when reading his poetry since he made so many claims for his own uniqueness, but it is a most necessary abjuration. The growth of a poet's mind, after all, does not take place in a propagator of his own devision, but in a world which is open to a range of influences and analyses unlikely to be implicated in the act of self-analysis. Nevertheless, Wordsworth's project in knowing himself was, to some extent, caught up with the belief that this was also the way to knowing humankind.

Thus far I have been concerned to suggest something of the complemenary relationship between Wordsworthian propaganda or manifesto and Wordsworthian criticism, and while this may be at the heart of the current status quo the situation is changing, and the need to resist Romantic ideology has been clearly and effectively demonstrated by Jerome J. McGann and Marjorie Levinson.[2] Because this is not a book that is solely concerned with Wordsworth, this is not the place for a full rehearsal of the changing directions of Wordsworth criticism.[3] Bearing responsibility for the risks of generalization, therefore, I would suggest that the orthodoxy or centre-ground I have described may now be weakening under the pressures of a new historicism that is concerned to disclose the complex processes whereby art transposes the actual into the aesthetic, not as a means of exposing the fallacious visions of fiction against the veracity of 'true history', nor to serve the cause of valorizing (in the way of Lukács) those works which best expose the conflicts and process of history. Rather, this movement is concerned to read against the grain of the promulgated (Romantic) ideology by locating an unconscious web of meanings and associations that inform the work in an essential way, but do not achieve status as subjects in the work's surface. In the case of Wordsworth, this involves getting behind the great system of transcendental or higher truth, and possibly subverting the holistic or affective systems which render the work complete

in meaning, to fracture the text at a point where its genetic
relations to the moment of its production may be exposed.
This historicism, concerned at it is with the process of the
aesthetic and not its evaluation, provides a way through the
philosophic and affective humanism which may be found in
Wordsworth and his critics. The alternative strategy of
deconstruction may be oddly less radical and disruptive here,
since so long as it refuses to arrest its continuous deflections
or postponements of meaning, it is only enabled to bring us
back into the inner circles of the Romantic dilemma or an
equivalent aporia.[4]

My study is far more restricted than the models to which I
have referred, and yet it will share the same ambition to break
open certain of Wordsworth's texts in the attempt to discover
the workings – ideological and otherwise – of a writing which
achieves the status and the functions of myth in the
Barthesian (or Marxist) sense of overturning the cultural into
the natural. In providing an alternative strategy to the
affective or philosophical critics, however, it is not my
concern to disavow the affective or philosophical
Wordsworth. Rather this is to be acknowledged as part of an
historical process (and not put down to originality or genius)
that is of great metamorphic power in Wordsworth's poetic
figuring of the world he knows or imagines to be real or
truthful. To begin with then, I shall place Wordsworth
within a theory of historical change which allows him to wear
the humanistic mask subsequently borrowed by his
commentators, by invoking the eighteenth-century change in
social relations described by Lawrence Stone as the rise of
affective individualism.[5] While Stone's thesis centres on the
family, and describes the shift away from authoritarian and
hierarchical structures which accompanied an increased
regard for the personal rights and feelings of each individual,
its pertinence to Wordsworth may be discovered in his
equivalent regard for individualism across barriers.
Wordsworth's humble rustics had as much right to ecstasy or
suffering as anyone else: as is well known, he saw them as
more emotionally mature, enjoying a special consonance with
nature, and offering a better model for the plain yet effective
language of communication than any other social group.

Moreover, his political concerns centre on the model of social organization that is central to Stone's thesis of changing relations – the family. The breakdown of family structure, the destruction of the rural domestic life and economy is for Wordsworth the collapse of the model of ideal harmony and mutual respect in which the human heart is properly cultivated. This is most clearly seen in the famous letter to Fox of 1801.

The poems with which I am chiefly concerned centre on these issues. As favoured examples of Wordsworth's romantic humanism, they are used to demonstrate his sympathies and belief in individualism. More consequentially, they are very pointedly poems about the fragmented family structure. *Salisbury Plain* (and the subsequent manuscript variations), *The Ruined Cottage*, 'The Sailor's Mother', 'Ruth', 'The Thorn', 'The Affliction of Margaret ——', 'Her Eyes are Wild', among others of Wordsworth's poems, are fundamentally concerned with lost husbands and lost children. The complete family is a consistently implied absence and implied forcefully too, by the feelings of the suffering woman: affective individualism here works through the tragedy of madness for the cause of the family.

The letter to Fox referred to above may tell us something of the origins of the early poetry, and because the extent of the political concern therein may surprise some readers, it is worth quoting:

In common with the whole of the English People I have observed in your public character a constant predominance of sensibility of heart. Necessitated as you have been from your public situation to have much to do with men in bodies, and in classes, and accordingly to contemplate them in that relation, it has been your praise that you have not thereby been prevented from looking upon them as individuals, and that you have habitually left your heart open to them to be influenced in that capacity. This habit cannot but have made you dear to Poets . . . .

It appears to me that the most calamitous effect, which has followed the measures which have lately been pursued in this country, is a rapid decay of the domestic affections among the lower orders of society. This effect the present Rulers of this

Country are not conscious of, or they disregard it. For many years past, the tendency of society amongst almost all the nations of Europe has been to reproduce it. But recently by the spreading of manufactures through every part of the country, by the heavy taxes upon postage, by workhouses, Houses of Industry, and the invention of Soup-shops &c. &c. superadded to the encreasing disproportion between the price of labour and that of the necessaries of life, the bonds of domestic feeling among the poor, as far as the influence of these things has extended, has been weakened, and in innumerable instances entirely destroyed.[6]

This represents an engagement with 'the real', a writerly attempt by Wordsworth to communicate a response to the social conditions he saw around him. The remarkable marriage to be witnessed at this point in his career is underway in this letter, the union between the writer intent on deliberately recounting a political reaction to what he feels is a social catastrophe on a national scale and the poet devising means of incorporating this reaction into a clearly specified and programmed aesthetic. Some readers prefer to see this not as a union but a divorce, and are prone to complain of the tyranny of the romantic aesthetic over political protest. They read Wordsworth anxiously, in search of the subdued but tell-tale signs of the political consciousness at work, either to condemn its subjugation, or to inflate the same subtle presence into a triumph of political integrity. Alternatively, the split may be described as that between the man and the poet, and this theory is frequently supported by a biography whose narrative is bent on stressing the victory of the maturing philosophical poet over the young and crude radical. Here we are back with the poet of the human heart and the eliding of the complex metamorphoses of politics into art.

Nevertheless, I shall be examining a phenomenon which submits in part to this biography, and shall argue that in the process that sees the tempering of Wordsworth's political poetry into a romantic aesthetic in the 1790s the figure of the deranged woman plays a crucial mythologizing role, and that oddly, in the development of the poetry of individualism, with all its altruistic concern, she becomes a most telling casualty.

II

I shall begin by quoting from a manuscript fragment entitled 'A Tale', probably written by Wordsworth between 1787 and 1789:

> Her dress, if you except a black hat (which bore no other marks than that of being drench'd in rain) tied by a dark green ribband which knotted under chin, was not much more warm or becoming than that of the poor, the lame, and the blind, who have no fire but the light of a Window seen at a distance, and whose candle is the little [———]. Her eyes were large and blue; and from the wrinkles of her face (which, from their fineness, seemed rather the wrinkles of Sorrow than of Years) it was easy to see they had been acquainted with weeping; yet had not perpetual tears been able to extinguish a certain wild brightness which, at the first view, might have been mistaken for the wildness of great joy. But it was far different – it too plainly indicated she was not in her true and perfect mind.[7]

This, one of the earliest pieces of Wordsworth's prose, represents the entry of the madwoman into the corpus of his writing, and at this moment an anxious yet rich source of inspiration is born whose impulses will continue to act across his entire career as a poet. Certain details – in particular the hat and its ribband, the garments of the lost life – recall Cowper's Crazy Kate, and if this is indeed the model, then the abiding concern in the poems succeeding the fragment is the cause of Kate's madness. For even while Wordsworth's deranged and deserted women are allowed only a limited amount of space to recount their histories, the details of those histories, sometimes if only in the form of indistinct traces, are almost always identical: insanity derives from desertion or bereavement and the hardship it brings, and sometimes from the loss of children. This fragment, however, indicates little if any of this kind of interest, and in so far as its slightness allows characterization, I would agree with the editors who suggest it may have been the beginning of a Gothic or sentimental tale. Whatever the nature of its project, this early experiment may be seen as the genesis of the figure with which this chapter is chiefly concerned – the female vagrant.

Most readers will know the female vagrant as the protagonist of the poem bearing that title in the *Lyrical Ballads*, but her textual history is both lengthy and complex. Her first certain appearance is in the manuscript poem known as *Salisbury Plain* written between 1793 and 1794, although Wordsworth himself later claimed to have written the episode of the female vagrant before these dates.[8] A manuscript (DC MS 7) dating from 1788 deals with a related theme, and Stephen Gill has suggested that it could have been revised into a version of 'The Female Vagrant' in a manuscript now lost. Together with the fragment quoted above, this evidence suggests a sustained series of attempts by Wordsworth early in his career to write a poem or tale about the deranged and deserted woman. The final appearance of the female vagrant is in *Guilt and Sorrow*, the revised version of the Salisbury Plain poems, compiled in 1841 and published in 1842, eight years before Wordsworth's death. Even after this, the relevant section of the poem received modifications in manuscript versions until 1847. From original inception to final version then, the history of this subject ranges across almost the whole of Wordsworth's long career as a poet.

Having written the manuscript poem *Salisbury Plain*, Wordsworth set about revising it in 1795 at Racedown and produced the text in manuscript known as *Adventures on Salisbury Plain* which subordinated the story of the female vagrant somewhat by an elaboration of the framing device. Attempts to publish this poem in 1796 and 1798 were ultimately unsuccessful, but what transpired was the publication of the *Lyrical Ballads*, for which Wordsworth lifted 'The Female Vagrant' from the manuscript. As a consequence, *Adventures on Salisbury Plain* (and perhaps by implication, the earlier *Salisbury Plain*) were left with large gaps in their centres. When still working on the poem in 1799, Wordsworth wrote that he intended to compose a new story for his wandering woman.[9] The gap in the manuscript, however, was never filled, and when Wordsworth finally published *Guilt and Sorrow*, he reluctantly replaced 'The Female Vagrant' at its centre, after further attempts to modify or replace her story.[10]

Wordsworth's meticulous habits of composition and

anxiety over versions of his manuscript poems are notorious, and some critics would regard it as specious, therefore, to take 'The Female Vagrant' as a special case. This may be fair warning but it is both tempting and worthwhile to ask particular questions about this figure who remained incomplete and on the edge of Wordsworth's poetical labours for most of his life. First and most importantly, is it the case that his manuscript gap was the curiously irritating absence that gave rise to the subsequent poems about deranged and deserted women, none of which found their way back into the original frame poem? If so, what was the nature of the fascination with this figure, that she proves so incompatible with the poetical context waiting for her? Second, is it the case that she occupies a crucial position in the development of Wordsworth's distinctly Romantic aesthetic in the 1790s?

The answer to the first question is probably yes. At least one poem from this group – 'Ruth' – was probably written for the specific purpose of filling the manuscript gap. But the similarity of theme and content in the others make them likely candidates or exercises in the same composition. So out of the Salisbury Plain poems come 'Ruth', 'The Sailor's Mother', 'Her Eyes are Wild', 'The Affliction of Margaret ——', and possibly 'The Thorn'. Here too we may find the genesis of *The Ruined Cottage*, and as a whole these poems constitute a nexus wherein we could also place the deserted women of *The Borderers*, 'An Evening Walk', 'The Forsaken', 'The Complaint of the Forsaken Indian Woman', 'Maternal Grief', 'The Emigrant Mother' and the much later 'The Widow on Windermere's Side'. From the discussions which perhaps surrounded the production of these poems, Southey could have taken his inspiration for 'Hannah', 'The Ruined Cottage', and his ballad 'Mary, the Maid of the Inn' (formerly and perhaps unfortunately titled 'Mary the Maniac').[11] The answer to the second question posed above is also yes, I shall argue, although the number of thematic preoccupations in this period, in combination with the different strands of Wordsworth's development, will not allow the importance of the deranged and deserted woman pre-eminence.

The significance of the woman's madness in *Salisbury Plain* may easily escape attention. To those familiar only with

'The Female Vagrant' it may seem a matter of contention
whether the woman is mad at all, since the version published
in the 1805 edition of the *Lyrical Ballads* (following the
manuscript change of 1801 sent by Wordsworth to Anne
Taylor) changes the line in which the woman confesses to
bouts of mental derangement.[12] This change is also preserved
in *Guilt and Sorrow*. *Salisbury Plain* tells the story of a
meeting between a traveller and a woman vagrant during a
stormy night. After strange visionary events the traveller
chances upon a shelter where he finds the woman moaning in
her sleep. He wakes her, and she tells part of her story until
daybreak, when they set off for a cottage in the distance while
she resumes her narrative. Here they receive sustenance, and
the poem then ends with a peroration on the unjustness of a
society which has caused the misery of such travellers,
playing upon the ironic juxtaposition of the historic and
distinctly pagan setting with that of the enlightened present,
and building to a climax in which the consequences of war
and tyranny are berated and the need for reform asserted. In
this context, the woman's madness is not so much an
opportunity for the exercise of sensibility as in Cowper's
poem, for example, or indeed, in some of Wordsworth's
subsequent examples, as it is a means of emphasizing the
social depredations to which she had been subject. As
Stephen Gill remarks of this text, the 'attack on the
oppression of the poor is the centre from which all of the
poem's questioning radiates' and, moreover, 'the oppression
of one female vagrant was suddenly seen to have intimate
links with the reasons why, for instance, the country was
plunging into an unjust war.'[13] This oppression finds its
ultimate tragic effect in the woman's madness:

> And oft, robbed of my perfect mind, I thought
> At least my feet a resting place had found.
> 'Here will I weep in peace,' so Fancy wrought,
> 'Roaming the illimitable waters round,
> Here gaze, of every friend but Death disowned,
> All day, my ready tomb the ocean flood.'
> To break my dream the vessel reached its bound
> And homeless near a thousand homes I stood,
> And near a thousand tables pined and wanted food.[14]

The loss of perfect mind (significantly the phrase comes from *King Lear*, and is also used in Wordsworth's early prose fragment quoted above) is here linked to details of the poem which need explanation. Madness here does not simply indicate an incomplete life, but is directly linked to an individual history in which specific events in late eighteenth-century England figure largely. These events – namely, enclosure, unemployment and the American War of Independence – combine to render the deserted or bereaved woman's position particularly precarious. It is in this context that her madness may be read, wherein it becomes the poem's way of marking how her right to a full Wordsworthian family life is denied.

For the woman's story is a detailed one. It begins with an idyllic evocation of a well-provided childhood wherein grazing and fishing rights supply humble but secure needs:

> 'By Derwent's side my father's cottage stood,'
> The mourner thus her artless story told.
> 'A little flock and what the finny flood
> Supplied, to him were more than mines of gold.
> Light was my sleep; my days in transport rolled:
> With thoughtless joy I stretched along the shore
> My parent's nets, or watched, when from the fold
> High o'er the cliffs I led his fleecy store,
> A dizzy depth below! his boat and twinkling oar.
>
> (226–34)

The fishing rights are subsequently denied by 'enclosure' ('His little range of water was denied' (258)) and the father's cottage possessed, probably due to pressure from larger landowners ('His all was seized' (260)).[15] Homeless, daughter and father turn to her young lover who marries her and provides for them both. She bears three children and her father dies at the moment at which the depression, and the American War begins:

> My happy father died
> Just as the children's meal began to fail.
> For War the nations to the field defied.
> The loom stood still; unwatched, the idle gale
> Wooed in deserted shrouds the unregarding sail.

How changed at once! For Labor's cheerful hum
Silence and Fear, and Misery's weeping train.
But soon with proud parade the noisy drum
Beat round to sweep the streets of want and pain.
My husband's arm now only served to strain
Me and his children hungering in his view.
He could not beg: my prayers and tears were vain;
To join those miserable men he flew.
We reached the western world a poor devoted crew.

                                        (293–306)

Although the details are slight, the references are particular. The shortage of food is directly related to the still loom, the cessation of the cottage cotton industries caused by the cut in American supply. In turn, this produces unemployment in this and related industries which subsequently creates a supply of men who may be easily recruited for the wars. Wordsworth gives no detail of the war itself, but its effect is the loss of the woman's husband and children, and her scanty narrative is doubtless meant to indicate her incomplete state of mind. She awakens 'as from a trance restored' (324) on board a British ship bound for home, and it is at this point in her story that she speaks of her madness.

The woman's story is thus a carefully contrived narrative into which Wordsworth draws the popular motif of derangement not for sentimental decorative purposes (therefore departing from Cowper's model) but for the purposes of constructing an individual history relating to contemporary events. The woman's suffering in *Salisbury Plain* derives from the real suffering of the rural poor in the late eighteenth century (indeed, Wordsworth claimed the narrative itself was drawn from life)[16] and it is here metamorphosed within the aesthetic which takes madness as the figure capable of representing this extreme suffering. In a way, what is conceivably economic reality is displaced by poetics, but the displacement itself relates in a most specific sense to the processes of history. It is a clever use by Wordsworth of a sentimental trope, for he converts the reader's stock sympathetic response into a reaction against social oppression. The woman is not a sufferer in 'natural' existence, but a victim of identifiable economic and political

events. The displacement of the poem is not an evasion of
history then, but a distillation of its events into one individual
life. Having achieved that, the poem moves appropriately out
of the woman's narrative into Wordsworth's peroration
which is equally precise in its identification of the
contemporary causes of misery: want of charity or proper
provision (435–8), dehumanizing labour (439–41), imperial
ambition (447–50) and war (505–13). It is from this
foundation that the poem delivers its revolutionary
conclusion:

> Heroes of Truth pursue your march, uptear
> Th'Oppressor's dungeon from its deepest base;
> High o'er the towers of Pride undaunted rear
> Resistless in your might the herculean mace
> Of Reason; let foul Error's monster race
> Dragged from their dens start at the light with pain
> And die; pursue your toils, till not a trace
> Be left on earth of Superstition's reign,
> Save that eternal pile which frowns on Sarum's plain.
>
> (541–9)

The metaphors used are the traditional metaphors of the
Enlightenment writers. After 1789, however, they attain far
more potent references.

When Wordsworth revised his manuscript in 1795 to
produce *Adventures on Salisbury Plain* this part of the poem
was excised in the course of a larger programme of alteration.
The cast of the original poem is widened, first by expanding
the history of the man who meets the female vagrant so that
his story becomes the poem's central concern, and second by
introducing more meetings and incidents. In Wordsworth's
words the new poem was concerned 'to expose the vices of the
penal law and the calamities of the war as they affect
individuals'.[17] This intention may still be read in the poem,
yet the alterations fragment (and by fragmenting, subdue) the
political energies of the first poem. Details of the revisions are
too numerous and beyond this study's concern to rehearse in
full, but I wish to draw attention to two main features. In the
first instance, the frame poem gains in stature by the
expansion of the theme of charity and mutual assistance. The

traveller (who had committed murder in his desperation) now meets an old soldier before discovering the female vagrant, and while this new figure embodies the hardship of oppression, the episode pushes more towards the significance of fellowship in the younger man's charitable assistance. This theme is continued and developed towards the end of the poem. Where *Salisbury Plain* points the reader towards a recognition of the exemplary hospitality found in the 'lowly cot' (415–24) *Adventures on Salisbury Plain* extends this section to include further scenes of mutual assistance so that the poem ends with the image of a rural society alleviating its suffering by way of self-help. Moreover, the reluctant impeachment of the murderer by the cottagers homogenizes their honesty and their duty to the state. In the second instance, the political energies of the poem are redirected to confront the barbarism of exhibiting the murderer's body after his execution. These two alterations are principal examples of a more general shift towards an assertion of human interdependence and mutual sympathy. Here the programme of the *Lyrical Ballads* is anticipated as the rural community is used as the locus for the 'essential passions of the heart',[18] rather than the section of the community in which the casualties of economic policy could be discovered. Significantly, it is in this new scheme of things that the female vagrant's story finds itself dislocated.

What then of its new context as a separate poem in the *Lyrical Ballads*? Now, the woman's tale is a history set adrift from its frame which was concerned to articulate an enlightenment and radical politics by means of its rhetoric and its allegorical setting. Certainly, the poem still retains its pointed references to the economic causes of deprivation, but the persona now stands alone, her voice and story now subject to the interpretative habits of readers who find her in the company of narrators like the ancient mariner and the mad mother, as well as those who are confused by their own stories ('We are Seven', 'Anecdote for Fathers', 'The Thorn'). In the first edition, then, the vagrant's story may be read as another example of the voice of suffering humanity, in the context of the second edition, with the *Preface*, as an example of the enduring and universal passions of mankind. Now her madness may indicate her incompleteness as well as the nature of her past, and this new context, wherein something of Cowper's sentimentality is recaptured for the services of a universalized notion of humanity, is extended to provide a basis for the successive poems on the same theme. If indeed these were written as exercises around the project of completing *Adventures on Salisbury Plain* then the dehistoricizing context of the new Wordsworthian aesthetic proves more alluring.

Two of these poems, 'Ruth' and 'Her Eyes are Wild' (originally entitled 'The Mad Mother') retain traces of the madwomen in the *Salisbury Plain* poems in that the tragic events causing insanity are sited in America.[19] The mad mother comes 'from over the main' (line 4) and survives partly (it is suggested) by a knowledge of the ways of the woods gleaned from the American Indians ('And I will always be they guide,/Through hollow snows and rivers wide/I'll build an Indian bower; I know/The leaves that make the softest bed' (53–6)). She is deserted, the poem implies, during her life in America, where her husband still remains ('far away', line 80). Her history, such as it is, shares characteristics with Ruth's, who is wooed by a soldier who had lived with the Indians in America, and Othello-like, charms her with traveller's tales into marriage. Whether the genesis of these curious details is to be found in *Salisbury Plain*'s identification of the American War as a nursery of social disasters, an equation also exploited in the figure of the deserted woman of 'An Evening Walk' (1793), or in the more Romantic version of America found in 'The Complaint of a forsaken Indian Woman' it is difficult to decide.

'Her Eyes are Wild' takes the form of a dramatic fragment unframed and unmediated by a narrative voice. In this respect it is seemingly a means of giving utterance to the trials of the mad and deserted woman. This poem, like so many others of the period, takes as its emotional centre the pathos of separation: the woman wanders in search of the husband who has left her (line 94), and her broken utterances are thus correspondent with the incompleteness of her being which the poem is bent on asserting. The woman alone is but a fragment of a whole life, and her existence here is tenuously held together by her integration with the natural environment which she believes will provide for her (stanzas 6 and 10) and the strength of her maternal love, most clearly realized in the therapeutic effects of the suckling child: 'Suck, little babe, oh suck again!/It cools my blood; it cools my brain;/Thy lips I feel them, baby! they/Draw from my heart the pain away.' (31–4).[20] Mary Jacobus once suggested that we have to 'read through' this poem 'to emotions it barely articulates'.[21] That is a very difficult project, and the most striking absence asserted in the poem is not an elusive emotion I think, but the husband. In giving voice to the woman by speaking for the woman, Wordsworth is effectively silencing her through the language of madness and obsession: without the man she is made to be lost, eternally wandering. Without the child (also male) the poem suggests the last remains of sanity would disappear. In fact the sanity here recognized in the woman's lucid interval is contiguous to the strength of her maternal emotion, which in turn is effectively defined by that familiar emblem of womanhood – the nurse. As the child removes himself from the breast, the mother is confronted with a vision of a more total madness:

> My little babe! thy lips are still,
> And thou hast almost suck'd thy fill.
> – Where art thou gone my own dear child?
> What wicked looks are those I see?
> Alas! alas! that look so wild,
> It never, never came from me:
> If thou art mad, my pretty lad,
> Then I must be for ever sad.

> (83–90)

Insanity is therefore separation: the more complete the fracture, the more complete the mental disintegration which follows. Freud too sees this as a traumatic moment: the husband's desertion after his sexual satisfaction is here mirrored in the poem by the action of the child:

To begin with, sexual activity attaches itself to one of the functions serving the purposes of self-preservation and does not become independent of them until later. No one who has seen a baby sinking back satiated from the breast and falling asleep with flushed cheeks and a blissful smile can escape the reflection that this picture persists as a prototype of the expression of sexual satisfaction in later life. The need for repeating the sexual satisfaction now becomes detached from the need for taking nourishment – a separation which becomes inevitable when the teeth appear and food is no longer taken in by suckling, but is also chewed up.[22]

I offer this not as a 'master text' against which Wordsworth's 'truth' may be registered (the common if discreet method of much psychoanalytic criticism) but as evidence of the deeply inscribed notions of womankind that pervade our systems of thought, or more correctly perhaps, find themselves easily replicated in the normal figures of our discourse. Freud and Wordsworth are at one in implying that the woman is in supplementary relationship to the man, whose absence, therefore, means the loss of the agent of definition. In Wordsworth's poem, so long as the child effects a kind of completion with his body through the act of suckling, some remnants of sanity remain. In Wordsworth's terms perhaps, these are the 'permanent passions of our nature', here quite simply maternal emotion. As the child removes himself, satiated (as Freud would say) the woman can only perceive a more permanent and endemic madness. It is therefore significant that the poem works around images of preservation and provision. While the mother retains the role of provider (line 50) she resists despair, and also retains the idea of a complete life in the act of sustaining herself and her son through the benevolence of a providential nature. The notion that she must be provided for – by husband or nature – overrides the distinction between them in the conflation of both towards the end of the poem: 'I know the poisons of the shade,/I know the earth-nuts fit for food;/Then, pretty dear, be not afraid;/We'll find thy father in the wood' (95–8). The father here may be read literally or metaphorically: symbolically, however, his relation to the woman is the same in each case.

'Ruth' too is actively concerned with provision. As a child Ruth's self-sufficiency is of a Rousseauistic anti-social kind,

as she moves away from society and her father to become
'herself her own delight', a child of nature:

> When Ruth was left half desolate,
> Her father took another Mate;
> And so, not seven years old,
> The slighted Child at her own will
> Went wandering over dale and hill
> In thoughtless freedom bold.
>
> And she had made a pipe of straw
> And from that oaten pipe could draw
> All sounds of winds and floods;
> Had built a bower upon the green,
> As if she from her birth had been
> An Infant of the woods.
>
> (1-12)

The politically symbolic landscape of *Salisbury Plain* is here
replaced by a landscape incorporating the romantic
metaphysic of harmonious nature, a landscape which will
eventually reclaim Ruth after her second desertion. This
childish independence is corrupted, the poem suggests, by
the lover who has lived with the ignoble savages in America.
Having inherited the 'wild men's vices' (line 143) he proves
untrustworthy, entrancing Ruth and then deserting her after
the marriage:[23]

> Meanwhile as thus with him it flared,
> They for the voyage were prepared
> And went to the sea-shore,
> But, when they thither came, the Youth
> Deserted his poor Bride, and Ruth
> Could never find him more.
>
> 'God help thee Ruth!' – Such pains she had
> That she in half a year was mad
> And in a prison hous'd,
> And there, exulting in her wrongs,
> Among the music of her songs
> She fearfully carouz'd.
>
> (163–74)

Here madness is seen as developing directly out of the loss of the man, and from this point Ruth is incomplete in herself. Her individuality disintegrates in her derangement: the singleness stressed in the third stanza is utterly lost in the fragmentary after-life of madness. It is true that after asserting Ruth's madness the poem directs itself towards the subject of her restoration, but this restoration is of a very particular kind, being concerned less with the woman's individuality than with the providential and life-giving universe she unwittingly inhabits. Upon escaping confinement and returning to the fields she finds a new freedom and perhaps a new kind of sanity ('The master-current of her brain/Ran permanent and free' (188–9)) and she partially redeems the innocence of her childhood existence in once again finding provision in the rural landscape itself and the naturalized humanity which populates it:

> A barn her *winter* bed supplies,
> But till the warmth of summer skies
> And summer days is gone,
> (And in this tale we all agree)
> She sleeps beneath the greenwood tree,
> And other home hath none.
>
> If she is press'd by want of food
> She from her dwelling in the wood
> Repairs to a road side,
> And there she begs at one steep place,
> Where up and down at easy pace
> The horsemen travellers ride.
>
> (199–210)

Yet if Ruth is the beneficiary of this naturalized providence, she is never wholly integrated into it. The 'oaten pipe' of her early pastoral life is discarded and replaced by the hemlock flute with which she solaces herself (lines 211–16) and her imitation of her childhood play is offered as the pathetic signs of the life forever lost, and not as the reclamation of innocence. When Ruth has escaped from confinement, the poem pulls in two directions at once, and both are removed from the political or historical concerns of the Salisbury Plain manuscripts. The sentimental possibilities of the insane figure unconsciously reliving the amusements of childhood (217–22) are irresistible to Wordsworth, while simultaneously he gives way to the attractions of a nostalgic or humanitarian depiction of a charitable self-helping rural community. Both work against the restitution of the woman's individuality, the one by indicating a relapse into helpless derangement, the other by disallowing economic independence.

Although the poem verges on topicality in its notation of the fact that Ruth as a lunatic of the rural lower orders finds herself in prison rather than an asylum, it veers sharply away from social commentary as Wordsworth places his madwoman after her release in a charitable rural society which, as 'The Old Cumberland Beggar' implies, was fast disappearing. The alienation of Ruth's madness, then, denotes a dissociation from herself, from cognition of the significance of her former life, and from participation in the social intercourse of the community, but not from humanity itself, which the poem merges with nature to produce an indistinct impression of Providence. This is confirmed by the poem's ending which envisages Ruth's absorption back into the community after her death in the Christian burial service performed by the local people, a spiritual homecoming of a kind which serves to connect the care she received in the natural world with that provided by God. Thereby the poem places its faith in a benevolent world order.

Ruth is the subject of her poem as the mad mother is the subject of hers. The former is the subject perceived through the impersonal and direct narrative of the ballad mode, while the latter is the speaking subject providing the utterances by which her history and state of mind may be read. In this way, these two poems are distinct from 'The Thorn' which places the distracted Martha Ray as object by its grammar: she is the thing perceived, the object spoken about. This hierarchy of subject and object governs the distribution of the poem's overt concerns, which are to chart reactions to Martha Ray and to investigate the psychology of the narrator's questioning, rather than to delve into the history which – of necessity in this arrangement – remains unknown. Consequently, Martha Ray is the most subdued madwoman, in a literal sense, in Wordsworth's poetry. Here no licence is given for the woman to tell her own story, and her utterances are reduced to the inarticulate repetitious signals of emotional abandonment – 'Oh misery! oh misery!/Oh woe is me! oh misery!' Martha Ray is virtually silenced where other of Wordsworth's distracted or deserted women are allowed speech, even if by way of interlocution that speech is ultimately enclosed by a listener's reaction. The placing of the woman's narrative within a structure of response or wider thematic interest, thus directing attention away from the history of events and towards the reception of that history is a growing tendency in the Salisbury Plain project.

The second version, *Adventures on Salisbury Plain*, transfers its focus from the woman's narrative to the significance to be found in its being heard by the murderer, and that growing interest is also to be witnessed in *The Ruined Cottage*, where the full significance of Margaret's story is pushed first into the wanderer's response and then the narrator's.

In the sequence of poems that deal with distracted or deserted women running from the original *Salisbury Plain* and the manuscript versions through *The Ruined Cottage* to the *Lyrical Ballads*, an interesting and possibly sequential series of experiments can be observed that are principally concerned with the relation of the woman's history. Seemingly, Wordsworth's vocational concern with the reception and interpretation of his poems by the public finds an aesthetic paradigm in the placing of the woman's narrative within a context created by a deep interest in the question of response and also that of wider philosophical significance. In confronting these issues Wordsworth finds himself presented with a choice: the woman's narrative can exist as a dramatic fragment ('The Female Vagrant', 'Ruth', 'Her Eyes are Wild', 'The Affliction of Margaret ——') or it can be cautiously and carefully placed within a system of relations designed to promote a 'proper' philosophical response, and one possibly also designed to investigate the psychology of response, as in *The Ruined Cottage*. If the *Lyrical Ballads* shows a tendency to favour the dramatic mode, then it also compensates for this somewhat in 'The Thorn', a poem which shares the monologue form, but attributes it to the person responding to the deserted woman. In this new scheme of things the woman's story is subjugated to the extent that it is not a story at all, but a history that may only be constructed by conjecture. She is given the voice of complaint, but no more, in the poem's complete concentration on the narrator and his reactions. In an odd sense perhaps, but a valid one all the same, this could be seen as Wordsworth's retreat to the aesthetics of Cowper's Crazy Kate, where history was almost irrelevant and response (sentimental response) everything. Here history is again a matter of guesswork, but the guesswork itself is now written into the poem.

So whereas elsewhere in the *Lyrical Ballads* Wordsworth gives prime subject position to the woman's voice or the woman's story, 'The Thorn' is at pains to subdue the woman's possible emergence as the subject. This emergence is possible because, in an obvious way, Martha Ray occupies the central position in the poem, and by allowing her to say so little, Wordsworth makes the perplexed fascination of the narrator the perplexed fascination of the reader. Evidence for the attempts to suppress Martha Ray's potential to disrupt the economy of the poem which takes as its subjects the narrator and the natural world in which he moves, may be found in a series of commentaries by Wordsworth, all apparently designed to suggest that the poem is about anything but Martha Ray. Initially, he claimed to have regarded the poem as a celebration of the awesome qualities mysteriously present in apparently ordinary natural objects. 'The Thorn'

> arose out of my observing, on the ridge of Quantock Hill, on a stormy day, a thorn which I had often past, in calm and bright weather, without noticing it. I said to myself, 'Cannot I by some invention do as much to make this thorn permanently an impressive object as the storm has made it to my eyes at this moment?' I began the poem accordingly . . .

The genesis of a poem may be distinct from the purpose an

author subsequently sees in it, however, and later
Wordsworth was to provide an alternative version of the
poem's design, stating that 'The Thorn' was to 'show the
manner in which such men [the narrator, a retired sea
captain] cleave to the same ideas; and to follow the turns of
passion, always different, by which their conversation is
swayed.' Here, obsession, passion and response to scenes of
suffering become the poem's subject. A third apology for the
poem occurs in Wordsworth's diagnosis of its rhetorical
technique. In this analysis 'The Thorn' may be recognized as
a typical early Romantic experiment in poetic language:

> Words, a poet's words more particularly, ought to be weighed in
> the balance of feeling, and not measured by the space they
> occupy upon paper. For the reader cannot be too often reminded
> that poetry is passion: it is the history and science of feelings.
> Now every man must know that an attempt is rarely made to
> communicate impassioned feelings without something of an
> accompanying consciousness of the inadequateness of our own
> powers, or the deficiences of language. During such effort there
> will be a craving in the mind, and as long as it is unsatisfied the
> speaker will cling to the same words, or words of the same
> character. There are also various other reasons why repetition
> and apparent tautology are frequently beauties of the highest
> kind. Among the chief of these reasons is the interest which the
> mind attaches to words, not only as symbols of the passion, but as
> *things*, active and efficient, which are of themselves part of the
> passion.[24]

Here the distance between the narrator and the poet
diminishes greatly as the speakers in the poem are now
regarded as unwitting poets. Of course, Wordsworth saw
many purposes in his poem: I am not quoting these extracts as
evidence of some kind of contradiction of intention, but to
demonstrate that in Wordsworth's willingness to confess a
variety of aesthetic projects at work within 'The Thorn', no
mention is made of Martha Ray as the possible subject or
centre. Initially, Wordsworth feels, the poem is about the
thorn itself, then about its narrator's obsessions, and then
about the language of passion. It is possible to see 'The
Thorn' as representing an odd interlude in the history of

Wordsworth's poems about deranged and deserted women. In one important sense the obsession of the poem is not the narrator's but Wordsworth's (as his repeated engagements with this theme testify) and if this is accepted, then the narrative method of the poem could be regarded as an act of displacement whereby the sea captain's bewilderment becomes the surrogate for the author's uneasy relationship with this recurrent topic in his poetry.

Faced with Wordsworth's accounts of the poem, not all his critics have taken him at his word, questioning the submerged position of Martha Ray in the poem's apparatus. The debate over the poem's real subject need not be summarized here, since such a summary may be found in James Averill's book. With typical acumen, Averill sees 'The Thorn' as 'an experiment upon the formula of *The Ruined Cottage*'. This is surely right, and there is no need to cite the parallels again. Averill's discussion leads him to confront the puzzle under consideration here which, as he shows, has been repeatedly encountered in the critical debate. 'It is most strange,' he writes, 'that, wishing to make the thorn a "prominent" object, the poet should dream up the story of Martha Ray, with its complicated machinery of narrator and listener.' Averill resolves the issue by reference to the aesthetic tradition which related sublime emotions to tragic feelings, following a similar path thereby, to Jacobus and Gerard, both of whom, as he notes, give notice of literary precedents for the relationship.[25]

My interest here leads me to suggest an alternative solution, for Wordsworth did not have to 'dream up' Martha Ray. She is yet another version of the female vagrant figure, a permanent presence haunting his inspiration in this period. The process of the poem, therefore, whatever Wordsworth's claims, can be seen as working in the opposite direction: it is not the sublime and the tragic which concoct Martha Ray, but the madwoman creating yet another setting for herself. Having dislocated the female vagrant from her original context, Wordsworth is still seeking a new, perhaps more aesthetic, context to replace the historical context lost in the operation performed on the Salisbury Plain manuscripts. Interestingly, the poem turns out to be about the impossibility of finding such a meaningful placing. Whereas *The Ruined Cottage* was able to accommodate and harness Margaret's tragedy through Armytage's equanimity and sagacity, 'The Thorn', in creating the narrator figure Wordsworth identified as a retired sea captain, absorbs the woman's story not into philosophy or worldly wisdom, but into the more confusing area of his obsessive and superstitious mind. The poem documents a state of mind that is unable to imbue the events and stories to which it is witness with meaning.

The poem opens up a gap between what the narrator knows and what he sees. This is also the gap between the thorn and Martha Ray: the association of symbol and person is posited but the precise meanings of this identification or parity are neither charted nor substantiated by consistent implication. In Wordsworthian terms the gap is there to be bridged or at least confronted in the act of reading. The 'deficiencies of language' to which he refers in his commentary on the poem are exemplified in the narrator's circular utterances which consistently invite the reader to construct a symbolic reading which identifies Martha with the thorn more fully. Such a reading would see her as a figure of permanent and inevitable natural suffering: ageless ('You'd find it hard to say/How it could ever have been young'), barren ('no leaves it has'), forlorn and wretched (see stanza 1). The moss which attempts to drag the thorn down (stanza 2) is probably the same moss adorning the infant's grave, its colour and vigour (stanzas 4 and 5) signifying the life that never was, the life that confirms Martha's madness as permanent. But of course, despite the hostility of the thorn's environment, 'it stands erect', and we are told this twice in the opening stanza. It somehow survives, alive, just as Martha Ray survives after the death of her sanity and spirit. Like Lucy (who is described by way of a symbolic or associational relationship with objects), Martha Ray finds herself characterized by objectification. Yet the objectification is never fully completed. The status of the violet, the star, or the thorn is equivocal in each case, and just as it is difficult to tell whether Lucy's relation to the single star in the sky is complimentary, so too the relation of Martha to the thorn is awkward and ambiguous. Does this confer her

with dignity or barren decrepitude? The poem's detail will
not provide an answer, and we are effectively warned off a
literal interpretation seeking a fuller history by the fact that
this is what the sea captain ('credulous', we remember) does
in answer to the intercolutor in stanza 20:

> 'But what's the Thorn? and what the pond?
> And what's the hill of moss to her?
> And what's the creeping breeze that comes
> The little pond to stir?'
> 'I cannot tell; but some will say
> She hanged her baby on the tree;
> Some say she drowned it in the pond,
> Which is a little step beyond,
> But all and each agree,
> The little Babe was buried there,
> Beneath that hill of moss so fair.'

Of course, these large elements of doubt are significant.
The female vagrant figure is having her history whittled away
to the extent that she is becoming a naturalized object within
the landscape. All that is known is that she sinks into madness
upon desertion by her lover, recovers in pregnancy, and
relapses again after losing her child. The reader's attempts to
make something of the poem's central vignette in which
Martha Ray stands next to the thorn and the mound must
therefore operate outside the limits of history or revealed
circumstance. He or she is left to juggle the three components
until they fall into some sort of ordered pattern or coherent set
of relations. One such reading has been ventured above, in
which the thorn itself is seen as an emblem of Martha's
suffering and endurance. Thus she is attributed with qualities
residing in the landscape to which she belongs in the same
way as Wordsworth's leech-gatherer. Alternatively, the
phallic qualities of the thorn might suggest the father, and as a
consequence, the juxtaposition of Martha, the mound and the
thorn may be read symbolically as a restored trinity of father,
mother and child. In part, such a reading would be an
explanation of Martha Ray's object-fetishism.

In both the emblematic and the symbolic reading the

woman's suffering is symptomatic of her incompleteness. This is most obvious in the symbolic reading with the thorn as father and the mound denoting the lost child, the absence of the family providing a coherent reading of Martha's incoherent and obsessive behaviour, and the thorn's barrenness suggesting the central presence of the phallus as governing symbol structuring the trinity but yielding nothing. In the emblematic reading, incompleteness is again suggested by the thorn, but this time its sterility reflects upon Martha.

In either case I take it that there is a stock unconscious formula at work behind the poem structuring its formal and symbolic relations, and the act of reading may take account of that formula in so far as it takes place within the broad ideological arena in which the woman is seen as supplementary to the man. This is not to defer to the dominant ideology, but to recognize its pervasive power and to expose it. Thus recognition of the source of the formula becomes all-important. Yet 'The Thorn' need not necessarily remain suspended within the ideology that produced it. A more radical reading might choose to produce a different meaning here by seeing the thorn itself as representative of the oppression to which Martha is subjected by way of its tyrannical presence in her obsessions. To move even further with an ideologically disruptive reading would entail a denial of the incoherence of derangement's language, and a stripping away of the pejorative implications of madness, so that Martha Ray emerges as independent in her new life. This reading is possible because of the open qualities of the text, enclosed not by knowledge, but the narrator's perplexity and lack of understanding.

A similar kind of ambiguous relationship between the deranged woman and the object with which she is associated is again present in 'The Sailor's Mother'. In this instance the ballad mode allows for an incomplete framing: the narrator simply offers a preamble to the woman's speech and no more. Again then, the presence of a narrative voice is ventured, but it does not seek to enclose the woman's utterances within its own wisdom or emotional response. Nevertheless, this voice serves to introduce the woman's suffering as heroic:

One morning (raw it was and wet –
A foggy day in winter time)
A woman on the road I met,
Not old, though something past her prime:
Majestic in her person, tall and straight;
And like a Roman matron's was her mien and gait.

The ancient spirit is not dead;
Old times, thought I, are breathing there;
Proud was I that my country bred
Such strength, a dignity so fair:
She begged an alms, like one in poor estate;
I looked at her again, nor did my pride abate.

(I–I2)

The sailor's mother steps out of the past, and is used by the
narrator as an anachronism, a means by which past glories are
evoked and present decadence or degeneration is implied.
The nostalgia locates itself in a common centre in
Wordsworth's poems of this period, that which is provided
by the idea of a lost world governed by the traditions of alms-
giving. Thus the woman is proud in her vagrancy, and
provided for by a charitable Community (for which the
narrator acts as substitute) that recognizes her status as
dependent in a way that paradoxically indicates her
independence. The protocol that is established here in the
narrators' response to the woman is endorsed and not
qualified by the poem's structure.

It is the case, however, that following this directive
preamble, the woman's brief narrative stands alone without
further interference, unframed by an additional response.
The voice which emerges may or may not be read as the voice
of madness, but it clearly illustrates obsessive behaviour.
Like Martha Ray, the woman identifies herself with an object
bearing the talismanic power to evoke that which is lost, the
caged bird reminding her of her son:

'The bird and cage they both were his:
'Twas my Son's bird; and neat and trim
He kept it: many voyages
The singing bird had gone with him;

When last he sailed, he left the bird behind;
From bodings, as might be, that hung upon his mind.

'He to a fellow lodger's care
Had left it, to be watched and fed,
And pipe its song in safety; – there
I found it when my Son was dead;
And now, God help me for my little wit!
I bear it with me, Sir; – he took so much delight in it.'

(25–36)

Here again the woman's relation to the object seemingly suggests an action which attempts to supplement loss by surrogate completion. But as in the case of 'The Thorn', the object with which she is associated may operate as a symbol or an emblem, and as the latter, the caged bird suggests the sailor's mother is imprisoned within her own obsessive grief. Either way her deranged or sentimental behaviour signifies the extent of the tragedy she has suffered, and that, in turn, takes us back to the conceptual habits that have such difficulty in realizing the woman alone as the woman complete.

In charting the movement between *Salisbury Plain* and the *Lyrical Ballads* and beyond, I have so far made little mention of *The Ruined Cottage*, a poem which is not directly implicated by or related to the problems and stimuli which issue from the removal of 'The Female Vagrant' from the *Salisbury Plain* manuscripts. *The Ruined Cottage* is not overtly a poem of woman's madness either, yet it bears a clear relation to the poems I have so far discussed in that it is a work intimately concerned with the deserted woman's grief and her degeneration. Moreover, it shares a common thematic interest with the *Salisbury Plain* poems in its relating of Margaret's decline to the conditions of slump and easy recruitment, and perhaps most important of all, as I have already indicated above, it is very probably the poem in which Wordsworth most thoroughly resolved the narrative difficulties experienced elsewhere. *The Ruined Cottage* enables him to place the woman's suffering most firmly into what he saw as a larger and more universal philosophical context, in its transition from MSB to MSD.

The framing of Margaret's story, after all, is perhaps the

most obvious feature of the poem's manuscript development,
and one which has attracted considerable critical attention.[26]
The centre of the poem – Margaret's grief and suffering – may
remain as the prime focus of attention, but the narrative
apparatus around it is a means of pushing its significance
away from Margaret's individuality and towards a resolution
which is both aesthetic (classically tragic) and philosophical.
The old man's speech to the disquieted poet, the mechanism
which patently directs the reader's response, is worth quoting
in full:

> The old man, seeing this, resumed and said,
> 'My Friend, enough to sorrow have you given,
> The purposes of wisdom ask no more;
> Be wise and chearful, and no longer read
> The forms of things with an unworthy eye.
> She sleeps in the calm earth, and peace is here.
> I well remember that those very plumes,
> Those weeds, and the high spear-grass on that wall,
> By mist and silent rain-drops silver'd o'er,
> As once I passed did to my heart convey
> So still an image of tranquillity,
> So calm and still, and looked so beautiful
> Amid the uneasy thoughts which filled my mind,
> That what we feel of sorrow and despair
> From ruin and from change, and all the grief
> The passing shews of being leave behind,
> Appeared an idle dream that could not live
> Where meditation was. I turned away
> And walked along my road in happiness.'[27]

The 'image of tranquillity' prevails, and 'uneasy thoughts'
and feelings are shown to be irreconcilable with the
meditation which is here a trust in nature and later in *The
Excursion* became more unequivocally a trust in God.[28] What
we are also witnessing here is that which *The Excursion* calls a
'trust . . . in controlling Providence' (VI, 560–1) and this is
something to which this later poem gives substantial weight
by way of the priest, the wanderer and the narrator. Here in
The Ruined Cottage it becomes the moral with which the
poem resolves its tragedies, and at the same time, a means of

negating the significance of the historical details to which the
earlier lines of the poem draw attention. For Armytage's final
speech re-translates the symbol of the ruined cottage itself:
where earlier in the poem it was the powerfully suggestive
symbol of the decay of the rural economy and family life in the
late eighteenth century, here concentrated in Margaret's
personal history, it now becomes converted into a more
poetically conventional symbol of mutability, the ruin of
time, which within the scope of Armytage's meditation, bears
consolatory remedies. Necessarily these remedies are of a dehistoricizing kind. The tranquillity of the ruin is larger than
its history, more powerful than the despair and grief which
the 'passing shews of being' bring. It is thus that history and
all its detail is denied.

Discussing the significance of this framing of Margaret's
story. Jonathan Wordsworth is right to stress that the
delicacy of the poem's composition ensures that the
resolution is undogmatic. It remains, nevertheless, as a
significant element in our reading, and not simply (as he
suggests) to make 'bearable a story which in its original
conclusion was too painful, too abrupt'[29] but unwittingly or
otherwise, to direct the reader away from the woman's
suffering and the disturbing questions which attend it,
towards a universalized scheme of things which enshrines the
values of equanimity, tranquillity, the stoic endurance which
witnesses and (it is implied) can feel suffering, yet rises above
its attendant hopelessness. Therefore, although Jonathan
Wordsworth and other approving critics have seen the
framing of the poem and its alterations from MSB to MSD as
an improvement, a purely aesthetic strategy, it is not just this.
It is the device by which Wordsworth mythologizes the
sufferings of the woman dependant, removing them from
history and placing them in a realm of experience provided by
Armytage's higher wisdom. What this venerable traveller
possesses in his knowledge is plainly that which Margaret
lacks. She is defined, therefore, in the wider scheme of the
poem, in terms of incompetence or lack of vision and truth,
and her suffering and degeneration is not so much of the poem
(MSD) as a subject for its discourse.

I have said that *The Ruined Cottage* is not a poem overtly

concerned with woman's madness. Yet it is possible to see it as intimately connected with the other poems I have discussed, differing only in its choosing to decline madness as metaphor or figure to signify the woman's degeneration after loss. The cottage itself fulfils that role. Indeed, it prefers to shift madness, or an allied condition, over to Robert, Margaret's husband, whose behaviour becomes aberrant during the slump which makes him unemployed. Nevertheless, some critics have chosen to see Margaret's mind as sick,[30] and while Wordsworth prefers not to grant her the language of manic or deranged obsession, it is clear that he regards her hopelessness as an undesirable abnormality in the scale of moral values provided by Armytage's meditation. Two surviving fragments from Ms versions of *The Ruined Cottage* known as 'The Baker's Cart' and 'Incipient Madness' confirm this and also suggest how the scheme of the poem at one time bore similarities to that of the *Salisbury Plain* manuscripts, and indeed, the later poems about mad women.[31] These rejected parts of *The Ruined Cottage* can only be placed alongside its early composition in 1797, and do not bear any obvious relation to specific extant episodes in the poem. Nevertheless, they can be recognized as experiments in exploring the states of mind that were eventually to be exemplified in the characters of Margaret and Robert. 'The Baker's Cart' is written in the first person and relates the scene of a baker's horse habitually stopping at the door of a household which can no longer afford to buy its bread. After a simple utterance by the mother ('that waggon does not care for us') the poet or narrator diagnoses the state of her mind as follows:

> The words were simple, but her look and voice
> Made up their meaning, and bespoke a mind
> Which being long neglected and denied
> The common food of hope was now become
> Sick and extravagant – by strong access
> Of momentary pangs driv'n to that state
> In which all past experience melts away
> And the rebellious heart to its own will
> Fashions the laws of nature.

Clearly, this kind of analysis was subject to considerable

tempering before it found its way into *The Ruined Cottage*, but the way in which it fits in with the poem's moral or philosophic scheme is obvious. The state of mind described is Margaret's – 'sick and extravagant', without hope, and rebelling against nature.[32] Here the woman's speech is minimized and subjected to an analysis that characterizes it as unnatural and devious in origin. 'Incipient Madness' (beginning incidentally like *Salisbury Plain* with the discovery of a hut on a moor, and therefore suggesting a close structural link between this earlier poem and *The Ruined Cottage*) deals with the obsessive behaviour of a narrator who returns nightly to a deserted hut to gaze at a broken piece of glass in the moonlight. The obsession, never fully explained, is nevertheless linked to a state of excessive grief:

> I cross'd the dreary moor
> In the clear moonlight; when I reached the hut
> I enter'd in, but all was still and dark –
> Only within the ruin I beheld
> At a small distance, on the dusky ground,
> A broken pane which glitter'd in the moon
> And seemed akin to life. There is a mood,
> A settled temper of the heart, when grief,
> Become an instinct, fastening on all things
> That promise food, doth like a sucking babe
> Create it where it is not. From this time
> I found my sickly heart had tied itself
> Even to this speck of glass. It could produce
> A feeling as of absence . . .

Again there is a hint of moral disapproval. Extravagant sorrow here supplants nature to become an instinct, and to create 'where it is not'. Nothing in this fragment betrays whether its speaker is a woman or a man, and although it initially seems most likely that it was originally meant to be spoken by a visitor to the ruin, the state of mind it describes is clearly not that of Armytage or the narrator. The obsession is more akin to Margaret's obsession with the cottage she will not leave. The odd symbolic object it chooses however has no counterpart in the manuscript versions of *The Ruined Cottage*, and it seems likely that this aspect of the fragment

found itself later directed into 'The Thorn' and possibly even
'The Sailor's Mother'.

These fragments indicate that the manuscript work on *The
Ruined Cottage* included elements and odd features which are
also to be found in *Salisbury Plain* and the subsequent poems
of women's madness – vagrancy, destitution, madness itself,
obsession. More importantly they indicate the ways in which
the two concerns of the poem (political and economic on the
one hand, and moral or philosophical on the other) may be
found in opposition. The deprivations of the poor in 'The
Baker's Cart' as in *Salisbury Plain* find a powerful emotional
lever in the deranged mind, its hopeless and distressed
condition providing a fitting analogy to the physical condition
in which it has its source. But in employing this device, 'The
Baker's Cart' finds itself disapproving of its moral
implications: it is self-obsessed and self-centred. Here and in
'Incipient Madness' the mental condition described is seen to
be one aggravated by a form of self-indulgence, even if
helplessly so. It is not that the protagonists are directly
reproved by the moral implications, but that their states of
mind are seen as deficient and possibly dangerous. It is left to
Armytage in *The Ruined Cottage* to retrieve this, for in a way,
his insistence on drawing wisdom out of suffering and his
measurement of moderation in sorrow stand as antidotes to
Margaret's despair.

Taking *The Ruined Cottage* and these two fragments
together with the Salisbury Plain poems, a common stock of
materials may again be found arranged in different
configurations. These include the slump and the rapid
decline of the rural economy, recruitment to the wars,
desertion, bereavement, loss, obsession, hopelessness,
destitution, madness or derangement, degeneration and
providence. Many of these, as I have shown, also figure in the
shorter poems of woman's madness written in the late 1790s
and the first decade of the new century. But *The Ruined
Cottage* and its fragments seem to be working towards a new
configuration wherein the woman's despondency is a kind of
unnaturalness, a rebellion against the values represented by
Armytage, and indeed possibly even a rebellion against
providence. So whereas the female vagrant's madness is a

temporary aberration caused by the extent of her suffering, and one which does not exclude her from provision, and whereas the mad mother, like Ruth, is the beneficiary of providence and her own fortified maternal emotions in her derangement, Margaret finds no provision, her excessive suffering brings on an excess of hope and desire that all but overturns her maternal role (she leaves the child while she wanders (320–9)) and ultimately this leads to total degeneration through self-neglect.

Margaret's story may be perceived in such a way as to give precedent to the moral tales of *The Excursion*, Book VI. Here the common components are again rearranged, but in a disengaged and less complex form. Madness is here reserved for the disapointed male lover (95–211) who regains sanity by submitting to a recommended therapy effected by God and Nature (176–96).[33] Woman's desertion and bereavement provide the centre for two separate tales: the first of a woman described in the Argument as 'an unamiable character, a female', and the second of Ellen, whose tragedy elicits the same reactions for the narrator as those experienced when listening to the version of Margaret's story included in the first book. The reference is significant, as too is the nature of the moral summary:

> For me, the emotion scarcely was less strong
> Or less benign than that which I had felt
> When seated near my venerable Friend,
> Under those shady elms, from him I heard
> The story that retraced the slow decline
> Of Margaret, sinking on the lonely heath
> With the neglected house to which she clung.
> – I noted that the Solitary's cheek
> Confessed the power of nature. – Pleased though sad,
> More pleased than sad, the grey-haired Wanderer sate;
> Thanks to his pure imaginative soul
> Capacious and serene; his blameless life,
> His knowledge, wisdom, love of truth, and love
> Of human kind! He was it who first broke
> The pensive silence, saying: –
>   'Blest are they
> Whose sorrow rather is to suffer wrong

Than to do wrong, albeit themselves have erred.
This tale gives proof that Heaven most gently deals
With such, in their affliction.

(1055-73)

Margaret's story may be evoked here for the purposes of
the poem's wider aesthetic and moral design, but it also
indicates a clear point of comparison, and suggests that the
elements of *The Ruined Cottage* are indeed being revised and
composed in a new form. Ellen, doubly bereft of lover and
child, seeks out her dead baby's grave, not to utter her grief
like Martha Ray, but as an act of penitential submission (a
'rueful Magdalene . . . penitent sincere/As ever raised to
heaven a streaming eye' (987-91). Her decline is meek yet
stoical:

> Meanwhile, relinquishing all other cares,
> Her mind she strictly tutored to find peace
> And pleasure in endurance. Much she thought,
> And much she read; and brooded feelingly
> Upon her own unworthiness.
> . . .
> - Much did she suffer: but, if any friend,
> Beholding her condition, at the sight
> Gave way to words of pity or complaint,
> She stilled them with a prompt reproof, and said,
> 'He who afflicts me knows what I can bear;
> And, when I fail, and can endure no more,
> Will mercifully take me to himself.'

(1025-48)

By way of contrast, the tale of the 'unamiable character' is
one of resistance and struggle against the conditions in which
she finds herself. The woman (in many ways one of the most
interesting in Wordsworth's work, anticipating Dickensian
figures like Miss Wade and Estella) is described as proud and
talented, 'surpassed by few/In power of mind, and eloquent
discourse' (676-7) and it is implied that she is ruined by her
'desire of knowledge' pursued in her youth by constantly
applying herself to study. As a consequence, the story
suggests, she becomes not obsessed but governed by ruling
passions. Wordsworth is seemingly regressing to more

traditional eighteenth-century models of humanity (and misogyny):

> 'Two passions, both degenerate, for they both
> Began in honour, gradually obtained
> Rule over her, and vexed her daily life;
> An unremiting, avaricious thrift;
> And a strange thraldom of maternal love,
> That held her spirit, in its own despite,
> Bound – by vexation, and regret, and scorn,
> Constrained forgiveness, and relenting vows,
> And tears, in pride suppressed, in shame concealed –
> To a poor dissolute Son, her only child.
> – Her wedded days had opened with mishap,
> Whence dire dependence. What could she perform
> To shake the burthen off? Ah! there was felt,
> Indignantly, the weakness of her sex.
> She mused, resolved, adhered to her resolve;
> The hand grew slack in alms-giving, the heart
> Closed by degrees to charity; heaven's blessing
> Not seeking from that source, she placed her trust
> In ceaseless pains – and strictest parsimony . . .
>
> (706–24)

Yet again Wordsworth places his solitary woman in a situation governed by trials of provision and maternal duty. But here her determination to resist becoming a dependant and entering into the exchange of charity (as giver or receiver) is seen plainly as a resistance against the scheme of things prescribed by God and the local society. The pastor uses this rebellion to exemplify the extreme limits to which divine mercy may extend (770–6). Although the woman's 'abnormality' is not madness, her mind is represented as perverted, and its potential sickness displaced into the literal detail of her illness, commencing at line 741.

These two tales taken together may be seen as a splitting of the complex paradox described in the discussion of *The Ruined Cottage* above – the paradox of Margaret's 'sickness' being simultaneously the result of deprivation and a degeneration enacted against the will of a providential scheme. Disencumbered of the device of madness or derangement, Wordsworth continues his study of the

deserted or bereaved woman and here divides Margaret's
history and psyche into two distinctly crude stereotypes. The
first woman develops the element of obsession from *The
Ruined Cottage* and its manuscript fragments into an open
rebellion against the providential scheme to which the moral
of Ellen's story would have her submit. She emerges as a
figure who will not accept the role of passive suffering
recommended by the poem's moral scheme 'indisposed to
aught/So placid, so inactive, so content' (730–1). Ellen adopts
Margaret's course of degeneration, but is seen as a figure of
enduring strength in her passivity. If *The Excursion* can be
accepted as existing in this sort of relation to *The Ruined
Cottage* than it is possible to use its simplifications as
indicators of the opposing attitudes at work behind the earlier
poem, opposing attitudes that in their deeply convinced
morality are kept largely in check by the text's refusal to enter
into homilies on Margaret's conduct. Even so, the traces of
such principles may be discerned.

III

The madness of the woman, set free from *Salisbury Plain*'s
historical placing, subsequently manifests itself in
Wordsworth's poetry in a number of different forms, his
narrative experiments moving uncertainly around this
recurrent topic. Whereas once madness served the cause in
which poetry and politics conjoined to enforce a recognition
of the typical rural casualties of late eighteenth-century
domestic and foreign policy, it later found itself engrossed in
a more distinctly philosophical and moral scheme set on
asserting the independence and necessity of human fortitude,
the instinctive roots of feelings, the homogenizing of
experience in the apprehension of a fundamentally
benevolent universe. In these new concerns, the common
pattern is that madness or derangement succeed desertion or
bereavement, and as a consequence easily ally themselves
with models of woman based on notions of mental frailty,
emotionalism, sentimentality and the inability to lead a single
life. While *Salisbury Plain* had partly deferred to such

models, it did not allow them to float unsupported, preferring
instead to render them as the consequence of a specific set of
historical circumstances. Quite simply, the original female
vagrant's suffering is not offered as a result of the inherent
conditions of womanhood, but as a result of her being a
particular woman at a particular time and place.

The same cannot be said of Martha Ray. Her place in the
poem in which she appears is that of a naturalized object,
undifferentiated from the other objects in the landscape. The
eccentricity of her placing, like that of the pond, the mound
and the thorn itself, suggests an odd natural configuration
unfathomable in terms of its history. Yet history is not fully
elided here, but replaced by a series of events derived from
the myth of crazy Kate: the woman is deserted; naturally she
goes mad. The precise nature of the conditions causing this
madness is never described, for the past now depends on
rumour or conjecture. Madness is the consequence of a life
elsewhere, only alluded to, never described. Oddly, *Salisbury
Plain* was written with the proclaimed aim of overthrowing
the habits of what it terms superstition; 'The Thorn' becomes
totally absorbed in the subjects which entertain the
superstitious mind.

Like other of Wordsworth's deranged women, Martha Ray
finds herself cast adrift into a timeless and ahistorical
landscape. Ruth, the mad mother, the sailor's mother and
Ellen inhabit a similarly vague world, but one which is also
characterized by its ability to provide for them even in their
suffering, through Christian charity, sympathy and support,
through the mysterious workings of providence, or a
combination of both. The significance of this derangement is
no longer to be found in the conditions of its creation, for the
new preference of the poetry is to delineate the world which
can accommodate it. Even while madness may still be used to
exemplify an extreme form of suffering or deprivation,
remarkable as such, its preference is constantly to push
towards a statement about the remarkable nature of the world
that responds to it. Thus the rural community that
Wordsworth wrote about to Fox is reconstituted in his poetry
to form a model of society able to rationalize or contain the
potential anarchy of madness within its charitable and

philosophical responses. Ironically, illness is used (particularly in *The Excursion* and *The Ruined Cottage*) to signify or characterize the essential health of humanistic response. Here madness may also serve the cause of 'deep and permanent passions' finding exemplification in the mother's love for the child. The deranged mind still gravitates to the rationality of the passions, to what Wordsworth takes as natural, the desire for the presence of the child or the husband.

Yet such is the nature of the figure of madness that the act of reading may choose to break up the ideological web in which it is caught and to reverse the formula which it seemingly represents. The irrationality of the woman may be read as extending to her passionate desire for completion and her dependency in such a reading now belongs to the false consciousness of the deranged mind. Given this volatility, it is perhaps not surprising to see Wordsworth attempting to shut down the play of meaning insanity promotes by framing his narratives or enclosing them within other devices designed to direct the response.

In the affective or philosophical reading of Wordsworth, the *Lyrical Ballads* and the *Preface* of the second edition are taken as documents declaring the strengths of Romantic humanism, and in the common judgement of this criticism the work of 1798–1807 is taken as evidence of poetic maturity. As I have suggested at the beginning of this chapter this judgement relies on a general if undeclared endorsement of universalism, a deep-seated belief in the validity of the poetry of experience. Consequently, a poem like *Salisbury Plain* fares badly in this body of judgement, and is seen as crude, polemical perhaps, and melodramatic. It is not my intention to reverse the judgement (I prefer to leave valuation out of it altogether) but to call into question the grounds from which it is delivered, and to suggest that the mad woman's movement through Wordsworth's verse follows a course defined partly by a tendency to fall back upon commonly available structures of thought and conception. So at the point at which Wordsworth's romantic achievement is usually acclaimed, which is also the point at which his radical human sympathies are usually sited – the *Lyrical Ballads* and after – we find a

developing aesthetic with preferences that tend to exploit
ideological myths about the natural and proper condition of
womankind. *Salisbury Plain* may not be a better poem than
The Ruined Cottage or 'The Thorn' but there are no grounds
for accepting it as a worse one excepting those which privilege
the poet's humanity and sagacity.

Wordsworth's romantic madwoman would appear to be
significantly different from her Augustan predecessor. For
Pope, Belinda's deranged behaviour in *The Rape of the Lock* is
a kind of self-indulgence, a vanity that his satire will set out to
correct. Yet at the same time (following Burton) he offers a
biological explanation that will leave womankind
permanently in the space occupied by his satiric intent: spleen
is the 'wayward Queen' who rules 'the Sex to Fifty from
Fifteen'.[34] What Pope terms 'the hysteric fit' is thus not
merely a behavioural aberration. Wordsworth seemingly uses
woman's derangement for entirely different purposes and
effects. It is now part of a tragic repertoire, attached to a new
class of experience which is unrelated to the obsessions
nurtured by an over-fastidious elite. Yet although no longer
linked to a specified biological condition (as in Pope's
reference to menstruation) it is fixed into an equally inevitable
history that probably depends on a submerged concept of the
woman's body, its functions and needs. This concept aligns
her normality with regular sexual intercourse, childbirth, the
presence of the child and providing for the child. To a
considerable extent, *Salisbury Plain* had played down such
notions, its social commentary limiting the play of
signification that woman's madness was likely to promote.
Once cut free from that commentary, however, the
derangement of the woman again alludes (however distantly)
to the 'derangèment' of her body, as she plays out her tragedy
in the theatre of cultural determination.

Notes

1. *Preface to the Lyrical Ballads* (1800), *The Prose Works of William
   Wordsworth*, edited by W. J. B. Owen and J. W. Smyser, 3 vols
   (Oxford, 1974), I, 134.

2. See Jerome J. McGann, *The Romantic Ideology: A Critical Investigation* (Chicago and London, 1983) and Marjorie Levinson, *Wordsworth's Great Period Poems* (Cambridge, 1986).

3. For this survey, see Marjorie Levinson (1986) for a particularly good analysis, pp. 1–13. My own analysis takes the force of this persuasive account.

4. Summarizing this, Levinson writes 'Wordsworth's poetry – with its reception protocols, its narrative contingencies, its reflexivity, its thematizing of figuration and desire, discourse and plenitude, repetition and reproduction – in short its irony and *aporia*, provided deconstruction theory with a perfect, that is, perfectly accommodating model of the literary. To put this more polemically, Romanticism's ideology of writing is deconstruction's ideology of reading.' Levinson (1986), p. 7.

5. Lawrence Stone, *The Family, Sex and Marriage in England 1500–1800* (London, 1977). See Chapter VI.

6. *The Letters of William and Dorothy Wordsworth*, edited by Ernest De Selincourt, second edition, revised by Chester L. Shaver, I, *The Early Years, 1787–1805*, pp. 313–4.

7. Owen and Smyser (1974), I, 7–8.

8. *The Salisbury Plain Poems of William Wordsworth*, edited by Stephen Gill (Hassocks, 1975), p. 7. For a full manuscript history, see Gill's excellent introduction.

9. See Gill (1975), pp. 9–10.

10. Ibid., p. 13.

11. For the connection between 'Ruth' and 'The Female Vagrant', see James H. Averill, *Wordsworth and the Poetry of Human Suffering* (Ithaca and London, 1980), p. 204. Wordsworth conferred with Coleridge on his revisions to the Salisbury Plain manuscripts to a considerable extent between 1796 (when Coleridge began his help in trying to find a publisher for the poem) and 1799. See Gill (1975) pp. 7–10. Coleridge also sent the manuscript to Lamb in 1796. Southey's poetry of the same period shows a sustained interest in similar subjects through such poems as 'Hannah', 'The Ruined Cottage', and 'Mary, the Maid of the Inn'. Although Coleridge had quarrelled with Southey in 1795, the common interest indicates the possibility of a common source, which must nevertheless remain a matter of speculation. We know too that Wordsworth read at least one poem of Southey's in manuscript in 1795. See Butler (full reference note 27), pp. 5–6.

12. See Gill (1975), pp. 121, 141.

13. Ibid., p. 5.

14. *Salisbury Plain*, lines 379–87. All quotations and references from *Salisbury Plain*, *Adventures on Salisbury Plain* and *Guilt and Sorrow* are taken from Gill's edition, cited above. Line references follow in parentheses.

15. See Gill (1975), notes to lines 258 and 261, p. 29.

16. Wordsworth's note to the female vagrant's narrative claims complete

veracity: 'All that relates to her sufferings . . . were faithfully taken from the report made to me of her own case by a friend.' Quoted in Gill (1975), p. 6 (note 12).

17. Ibid., p. 7.

18. *Preface to the Lyrical Ballads* (1800), Owen and Smyser (1974), I, 124.

19. Quotations and references from 'Her Eyes are Wild' ('The Mad Mother') and 'The Thorn' are taken from *Lyrical Ballads*, edited by R. L. Brett and A. R. Jones (London, 1963). Those from 'Ruth' and 'The Sailor's Mother' are taken from *The Poetical Works of William Wordsworth*, edited by E. de Selincourt, second edition, 5 vols (Oxford, 1952).

20. For a commentary see Alice Goodman, 'Wordsworth and the Sucking Babe', *Essays in Criticism*, 33 (April 1983), 108–25.

21. Mary Jacobus, *Tradition and Experiment in Wordsworth's Lyrical Ballads (1798)* (Oxford, 1976), p. 197.

22. Sigmund Freud, *On Sexuality. Three Essays on the Theory of Sexuality*, translated under the general editorship of James Strachey, edited by Angela Richards, *The Pelican Freud Library*, Vol. 7 (Harmondsworth, 1977), p. 98.

23. An interesting commentary on this poem (and the Othello parallels within it) may be found in Averill (1980), pp. 204–7.

24. De Selincourt (1952), II, 511–3.

25. Averill (1980), pp. 178–9. Averill's perceptive commentary is relevant here. See pp. 166–80.

26. See, for example, Jonathan Wordsworth, *The Music of Humanity: A Critical Study of Wordsworth's Ruined Cottage* (London, 1969), pp. 87–120.

27. *The Ruined Cottage* (MS.D), lines 507–25. References and quotations to this poem are taken from MS.D as found in *The Ruined Cottage and The Pedlar by William Wordsworth*, edited by James Butler (Hassocks, 1979). Quotations and references from 'The Baker's Cart' and 'Incipient Madness' are also taken from this edition. In all cases line references follow in parentheses.

28. See *The Excursion*, I, 951–6.

29. Jonathan Wordsworth (1969), pp. 5–9.

30. See, for example, Butler (1979), pp. 5–9.

31. Ibid., pp. 6–7.

32. I am indebted to James Butler's thorough editing here. See his comments on Margaret's relation to the states of mind represented in these fragments. Ibid., p. 6.

33. De Selincourt (1952), Vol. 5. All references and quotations from this poem are taken from this edition, and line references follow in parentheses.

34. *The Rape of the Lock*, IV, 57–8. For a summary of Burton's theory of women's 'vapours' in *The Anatomy of Melancholy*, see Vieda Skultans, *English Madness: Ideas on Insanity 1580–1890* (London, 1979), pp. 79–80.

CHAPTER FOUR

Secret Lives:

Sense and Sensibility, The Bride of Lammermoor, Wuthering Heights, Great Expectations

My previous chapters have attempted to show among their other concerns that the constructions of the meanings of woman's madness work largely by antithetical allusions. Thus madness is the opposite of the normal, the reasonable, the socially acceptable, and if Foucault's theory of madness in the age of reason is deferred to, then the eighteenth century (in which the romantic rhetoric of woman's madness is rooted) was largely responsible for consolidating this system of relations. Woman's madness then, is a means of defining *the* woman, and to seek out this definition in the texts of the past is an historical reading of ideology, an uncovering of a familiar phallocentric code. Yet, as is commonly accepted, the production of textual meanings is always cultural, and ideological history is an interested history of the present, not a disinterested history to reconstitute an 'authentic' past, for this is an impossibility. The critical means of the present, therefore, are drawn from a current cultural fund, permitting a contemporary relocation of textual meanings. This version of things may be too overdetermined for some, and it does not easily allow me to concede to the idea of the specifically female voice of the woman author, so distinct from that of the male in its capacity to open up structures within the text itself that are capable of unweaving its surface meanings, surface meanings that bear the outward marks of the patriarchal economy of sexual relations. My interest here is to make a return journey through these texts to locate the proposed definition of the woman, but then to return again to the conditions of the present, in which such a definition perhaps, should have no real currency.

Therefore I am resisting the path offered by such critics as Sandra Gilbert and Susan Gubar, partly because the universalizing implications of the woman writer's special insights are problematic for me, and partly because as a man I do not wish to make bogus claims for my own special insight into woman's special insights and practices. The nature of the essential difference of the woman's text cannot be mine to demonstrate. Nevertheless, of the six novels considered in these chapters, four are by women, and the hypothesis that woman's madness is recognized by woman authors as offering a specially appealing state capable of disrupting common assumptions and orthodoxies presents itself for consideration, and who could deny that Jean Rhys's *Wide Sargasso Sea* bears all the evidence to support this? This, however, is not an easy route for me to follow, nor am I anxious to strain the plausibility of this assertion by seeing all texts written by women in this way. What I wish to do may yet not be so distinct in its methods from the enterprise of Gilbert and Gubar. In seeing the text as mysteriously volatile in what it holds within a conventional (patriarchal) facade, they trace the source of that volatility to the (woman) author, whereas my suggestion is that it lies in the trope of woman's madness itself. The grammar of the text, its arranging the elements of meanings in relation to one another is peculiarly confused once the figure of the mad or deranged woman is let loose among those relations, a confusion possibly due to the double negative drive of madness and womanhood against what is really only a single positive of normality – for to say masculine normality would be to introduce a superfluity into partiarchal structures of rhetoric.

Current feminist debate requires a special interest to be taken in this rhetorical instability, for if its method of antithetical definition is always in danger of deconstructing itself, or offering itself for deconstruction, it is perceived in some way as a failure, and part of that failure is to fix or denote the proper actions and locus of woman's desire. What is left is a silence, a gap swallowing up the project of defining normality, to make way possibly, for a plural complex of being or sexuality, or one that is somehow not determined by the symbolic order of the phallus. In the intriguing eccentricity of the trope then, may be seen the mirror-image of the contemporary feminist project which works largely through the Lacanian revision of psychoanalysis to characterize woman without reference to the practice and theories of masculine sexuality, to escape from the Freudian paradigm which places woman by reference to the phallus by way of recognizing (as indeed did Freud) that sexual difference is a social and symbolic construct. Irigaray's way out of this is by defining the woman's body so that neither clitoris nor vagina are realized in phallic terms (as miniature or receptacle respectively) and so that the plurality of her sexuality need have no specific site: 'the geography of her pleasure is much more diversified, more multiple in its differences, more complex, more subtle than is imagined – in an imaginary centred a bit too much on one and the same. . . . "She" is indefinitely other in herself.' To escape the tyrannies of the ready-made formulae placing woman in relation to man, Irigaray argues:

> One must listen to her differently in order to hear an *'other meaning' which is constantly in the process of weaving itself, at the same time ceaselessly embracing words and yet casting them off to avoid becoming fixed, immobilized.* For when 'she' says something, it is already no longer identical to what she means.[1]

The other meaning of woman's madness that may be listened to in the texts discussed in this chapter is partly realized in her silence, her withdrawal, or her alternative language. While the surface meaning reveals the ideological history of the traditional symbolic order, there are other meanings to be found, meanings which find their way through a contest of language or styles set up within the novels themselves. In order to trace these, I will be using the methods of close readings.

One more aspect remains to be discussed as part of this preamble. The women of this chapter are distinct from others discussed in this book in that they all (with the exception of Mrs Gargery whose imbecility will be paralleled with Miss Havisham's derangement) suffer as virgins. In a very literal sense they do not pass through the ceremony sanctifying their entry into the phallic order, and while they are placed in the terms of that order symbolically, their own desires and fantasies may be retrieved from it as denotations of their secret lives, their own volitions, perhaps even their autoeroticism. The main symbolic threat to those private arenas, as will be shown, is writing, the letter or the marriage contract. Madness or derangement ensues as the woman refuses to accept the authenticity of the written word or its commands, and may be realized therefore, not as a collapse before a powerful order, but an equally powerful and independent alternative order, and not necessarily one defined by the nature of its opposition.

In Chapter 29 of Jane Austen's *Sense and Sensibility*, Marianne is discovered by her sister, Elinor, 'stretched on the bed, almost choked by grief, one letter in her hand, and two or three others lying by her.' Betrayed by Willoughby, bereft of a future conjoined existence, she lies broken amidst the remnants of her recent past. The letters, so important in *Sense and Sensibility*, denote the promised contact between the woman and her lover, and their scattering – as in Francis Danby's famous painting, *Disappointed Love* – indicates the dessication of what is tacitly posited as being a normal, whole, fulfilled and sane life.[2]

Marianne clearly is not mad, but Jane Austen's presentation of her leaves us in no doubt that she is suffering from a temporary derangement brought on by excessive grief. Whereas her separation from Willoughby earlier in the novel is presented unsympathetically ('Marianne would have thought herself very inexcusable had she been able to sleep at all the first night after parting from Willoughby' (p. 110)) and her conduct here explained by the fact that she was 'without any desire of command over herself' (p. 109), the final separation brought about by her receipt of his letter engenders a remarkable modal shift in the authorial voice. On placing her letters in Elinor's hands, Marianne 'covering her face with her handkerchief, almost screamed with agony' in an 'excess of suffering' (p. 195). In urging self-control and the need to consider her mother's misery, Elinor is told:

'I cannot, I cannot, . . . leave me, leave me, if I distress you; leave me, hate me, forget me! but do not torture me so. Oh! how easy for those who have no sorrow of their own to talk of exertion! Happy, happy Elinor, *you* cannot have an idea of what I suffer.' (pp. 197–8)

No wry authorial commentary follows. An ironic context can be found for Marianne's outburst in Elinor's reply, which suggests something of her own emotional condition ('Do you call *me* happy, Marianne? Ah! if you knew!') and in such a context Marianne's grief will be read as self-absorption of a kind, an introversion precluding knowledge or awareness of others. Yet in Chapter 29, this moral commentary finds itself in contest with the dramatic mode into which the narrative shifts. Here Jane Austen writes in a manner more commonly associated with the Brontë sisters when describing Marianne's actions and providing her utterances. Thus while the reader is not allowed to forget how her expression of her sorrows contrasts with Elinor's stoical reticence, Marianne's suffering is established as intense and beyond the bounds of reproach or moral commentary. What has pushed Jane Austen into this uncharacteristic narrative mode is her subject, sensibility, but more particularly, the locating of that subject in the romantic myth of the deserted woman's derangement. There is no insanity here, but in its place come closely associated behavioural abnormalities such as self-neglect, self-forgetfulness and emotional abandonment. In the medical discourse of the day, as I have shown, these were symptoms of mental instability, and in Jane Austen's novel, they are combined with a serious illness.

Marianne's illness, of course, is not the direct consequence of her disappointment, but the result of getting her feet wet in one of her solitary rambles at Cleveland. Nevertheless, the text allows the severity of her malady to be partially explained by 'the many weeks of previous indisposition which Marianne's disappointment had brought on'. The theory comes from Mrs Jennings, and is given some credibility in Elinor's response, which feels 'all the reasonableness of the idea' (p. 309). This illness therefore compounds the effect of her being jilted by Willoughby as she becomes the emblem of specifically feminine weakness, drawn close to death in her inability to endure life without her lover. Yet before she falls physically ill, she exhibits quite serious symptoms, far beyond distraction or mere self-indulgence. The course of her gradual discovery of Willoughby's deception is attended by a series of behavioural transitions increasing in their gravity.

After Willoughby's failure to arrive at Sir John Middleton's ball shortly after the Dashwood sisters arrive in London, Elinor (whose judgement the reader is encouraged to endorse) has 'fears for the health of Marianne' who is 'too restless for employment, too anxious for conversation' and walks 'from one window to the other' or sits before the fire 'in melancholy meditation' (p. 186). After a few days she is recognizably a melancholic, being now 'wholly dispirited, careless of her appearance' and indifferent we are told, in her feelings, 'lost in her own thoughts and insensible of her sister's presence' (p. 189). Shortly after this her restlessness is so developed as to prevent her 'from remaining in the room a moment after she was dressed . . . requiring at once solitude and continual change of place'. It is at this point that Jane Austen uses the language of contemporary medical writings when Marianne responds to her sister's soothing gestures 'with all the eagerness of the most nervous irritability'.[3] The contemporary reader would have been left in no doubt that Marianne's condition was extremely unstable. During this phase of her derangement, Marianne moves through the novel untouched largely by Jane Austen's (or Elinor's) censure, and the reader is further persuaded to a serious recognition of her grave state by the impropriety of Mrs Jenning's frivolous and teasing responses. It is only later that she becomes subject to the criticism which emanates from the novel's centralized moral values, and significantly, this criticism is not concerned to diminish her condition and its behavioural consequences, but is directed against her 'impropriety' and 'imprudence' in writing so familiarly to Willoughby (p. 200).

Sense and Sensibility presents Marianne's condition after her betrayal as an 'affliction' (p. 221) which it is not prepared to dismiss or undermine, whatever its final judgements on her emotional impetuosity. This is important to recognize because the novel sets out to classify behaviour, and it is therefore essential to understand what is genuine and what is not. Ultimately, the text will ennoble Elinor's silent endurance and correctness at the expense of Marianne's extravagance, but this hierarchy is not simplistically asserted at any point, and just as Marianne's warmth has its moments, so too her sensibility is accorded the serious regard that attends the afflicted state of derangement and melancholy. At the same time, however delicate and subtle Jane Austen's handling of the opposition proposed by her title may be, it remains an opposition played out in the structure that ultimately valorizes Elinor's strength against her sister's weakness, this weakness being exemplified in her derangement and subsequent illness. Thus while the novel is determined upon asserting woman's fortitude and independent capacity for self-control even within the social conditions which continually militate against such qualities (through Elinor), it seems it can only do this by developing the Dashwood sisters in antithetical relation, and therefore it allots an equivalent weighting to Marianne's frailty. Moreover, it associates this frailty with her unwillingness to accept the social conditions in which she finds herself. Marianne's radical capacity for asserting her desire is in this way denied as a strength, and her breaches of protocol are commonly represented as irrational and myopic, rather than challenges to the codes by which most of the other characters abide. The seriousness of her illness is enlisted in the cause of the seriousness of her weakness. Even while *Sense and Sensibility* represents Elinor as an embodiment of woman's strength, it fortifies that strength by way of woman's weakness, here yet again caught up in the myth of the betrayed woman's derangement. It is perhaps because of the antithetical relation of Elinor to Marianne that the potential insecurity of the rhetoric of derangement is largely played down in this text. Marianne's opposite and agent of definition, is a woman and not a man, and consequently, the retreat into self that characterizes her hysteric reaction is not one which creates a clear space for re-definition. The 'scream at the centre of the novel' which has attracted so much critical attention, nevertheless, is testimony to some sort of threat to this orthodoxy.

Marianne Dashwood's derangement may signify the incompleteness of the deserted woman, but it goes no further than this, unlike the later disappointed women with whom this chapter is concerned. Lucy Ashton, Catherine Earnshaw and Miss Havisham are all metamorphosed in their deranged states, entering new worlds of being in which their former lives and hopes are preserved in fantasies of desire or revenge. Lucy Ashton, in *The Bride of Lammermoor* undergoes perhaps the most startling transformation. She begins the novel as an incarnation of Pygmalion's fantastic desires, easily loved in her compliance, and ends as a revengeful maniac, killing the husband she is forced to marry in a violent fit of madness. Scott is at great pains to delineate and analyse the character of Lucy at the beginning of his novel, and in order to understand the relation of Lucy's madness to her former life, it is necessary to note the devices used in the early phases of the text.

It seems (not unnaturally) that Scott is intent on creating a heroine who will draw his readers' sympathy and excitement, for he begins by trading on clichés of feminine 'virtue':

> Lucy Ashton's exquisitely beautiful, yet somewhat girlish features were formed to express peace of mind, serenity, and indifference to the tinsel of worldly pleasure. Her locks, which were of shadowy gold, divided on a brow of exquisite whiteness, like a gleam of broken and pallid sunshine upon a hill of snow. The expression of the countenance was in the last degree gentle, soft, timid, and feminine, and seemed rather to shrink from the most casual look of a stranger than to court his admiration.[4]

Much is made in this section of the text of Lucy's passivity, of her child-like qualities, her modesty and reserve. From this demonstration of virginal purity and innocence, Scott moves into a rather more complex psychological analysis:

> But in her exterior relation to things of this world, Lucy willingly received the ruling impulse from those around her. The alternative was, in general, too indifferent to her to render

resistance desirable, and she willingly found a motive for decision in the opinion of her friends which perhaps she might have sought for in vain in her own choice. Every reader must have observed in some family of his acquaintance some individual of a temper soft and yielding, who mixed with stronger and more ardent minds, is borne along by the will of others, with as little power of opposition as the flower which is flung into a running stream. It usually happens that such a compliant and easy disposition, which resigns itself without murmer to the guidance of others, becomes the darling of those to whose inclinations its own seem to be offered, in ungrudging and ready sacrifice. (p. 27)

This description is built upon the stock-in-trade materials used by so much eighteenth-century literature in its depiction of women. In the preceding paragraph we are given an account of Lucy's romantic taste in reading (so frequently a part of woman's legendary impressionability) and the passage above begins with a reiteration of the characterization with which Pope opens his second *Moral Essay*. Even while Lucy may incorporate characteristics so gleefully exploited by generations of satirists before Scott, she is, of course, far from being an exercise in satire. In fact, these common elements are now being used as a means of making her attractive and appealing in terms of the values of the day. In itself, this demonstrates something of the ideological proximity of satiric animus to inconolatry where this image of woman is indulged. Lucy, 'matter too soft' sacrifices herself to those around her, becoming the receptacle of their particular interests, and thereby gaining their love (which Scott astutely diagnoses as narcissistic in kind). Her malleability is initially offered as a virtue, as she takes on the role of the assenting and even-tempered heroine.

Yet the plot will also work against the institution of these characteristics as virtues, for it uses Lucy's impressionable nature as a means of holding her partially responsible for the ensuing tragedy, and possibly even her own madness. For Lucy has a secret life, wherein her own desires and delights are exercised. Her clandestine pleasures are given considerable emphasis early in the text:

Left to the impulse of her own taste and feelings, Lucy Ashton
was peculiarly accessible to those of a romantic cast. Her secret
delight was in the old legendary tales of ardent devotion and
unalterable affection, chequered as they so often are with strange
adventures and supernatural horrors. This was her favoured
fairy realm, and here she erected her aerial palaces. But it was
only in secret that she laboured at this delusive though delightful
architecture. (pp. 26–7)

Yet as this demonstrates, Lucy's secret life is something to
which the text will not accord serious status. Her
acquiescence to those around her, her pleasure in pleasing
and her deference to the family hierarchy are all ways of
establishing her as a serious moral presence, an index by
which other characters may be judged. Her secret life,
however – particularly in the early parts of the novel – serves
to deflect the narrative into the well-established convention
wherein the unsteadiness of the woman's independent
imaginative life is confirmed. This shift is all the more
casually achieved because of the ready availability of the
satiric formula. The ultimate but tacit reference is to what
women do on their own, and that, the text implies, is
insufficiently important alongside the supportive or
complementary role. Nevertheless it is in the construction of
this orthodox satire that the dimension of Lucy's
independence begins to emerge. It is here, in the unlikely
setting of a commonplace misogynistic formula, that a gap in
the text can be located in which the concept of woman's
autonomy, and perhaps her autoeroticism, may be planted.
For the ultimate reference is indeed to the pleasures of the
self, and those need not be read as supplementary.

Because of this deflection *The Bride of Lammermoor* always
retains the potential to moralize upon the procedure and
events of its romantic plot. That is to say that Lucy's
clandestine meetings with Ravenswood and her final act of
revenge may be ultimately explained in terms of her
character. Her suspect tastes in reading and the resultant
fantasies may be clearly linked to her romantic desires and
loyalties. This pattern, after all, is a very common
arrangement exploited by any number of moral fictions to

indicate the dangers of an injudicious education or simple bad habits. In Scott's text, the evolution of tragic events is not fully endorsed by the narrative modes or the topos of the romantic and imaginative woman. These and closely related fictive devices have the effect of pushing the reader back into historical and deterministic explanations of Lucy's unfortunate end that are based in her character.

Sense and Sensibility offers its reader a similar historical analysis of Marianne's behaviour, but as I have shown, the novel is unequivocal in its representation of her grief. In an analogous way, but less securely, *The Bride of Lammermoor* sets its romantic plot in opposition to the 'common-sense' analysis of Lucy by giving such weight to the tragedy, and much of that emphasis is gained by the exploitation of the myth of the deserted woman's madness. Here that myth is implanted in a network of social relations, and in order to analyse its effects, this network needs to be set out in conjunction with its place in the plot.

Lucy Ashton is indulged by her father and despised by her mother. Her father's love is introduced as narcissistic ('it usually happens that such a compliant and easy disposition . . . becomes the darling of those to whose inclinations its own seem to be offered' (p. 27)) and the strength of this affection sometimes promotes what the text terms 'an unusual emotion' (p. 27). Her father tolerates Lucy's secret life, but he is not admitted to it. She is loved by her brothers but her mother is disappointed by her 'lack of spirit' and 'feebleness of mind' which she attributed to the 'plebian blood' of her father. She proposes to marry Lucy to someone 'whose ambition is of as low an order' (p. 28). She finds such a figure in Bucklaw with whom she arranges a match, but Lucy has already formed a clandestine relationship with Ravenswood, an enemy of her family. This liaison is ultimately revealed, and because Ravenswood leaves the area and does not communicate with Lucy, she finally allows herself to sign the papers betrothing her to Bucklaw, thus conceding to her mother's demands. Ravenswood returns minutes too late; Lucy's behaviour becomes erratic, and on her wedding night she stabs her husband in a fit of insanity, recovers neither reason nor strength, and dies.

This peculiar configuration is composed of strong and weak characters who supplant each other in their successive relations to Lucy. It is possible to elucidate these relationships by employing a Freudian model, but I do this cautiously, not to claim some kind of psychoanalytical 'truth' for the text, but to initiate a connection between two modes of writing (Scott's fiction and Freud's writings) that will be developed in the final chapter of this book. Lucy is dominated by her strong mother who wishes to replace her weak father – Lucy's love-object – with Bucklaw (weak). Secretly, however, Lucy attaches herself to Ravenswood (strong) thereby achieving two aims: first she releases the repressed love for her mother by replacing her dominance by that of Ravenswood; second, she frees herself from her (anxious) incestuous desires for her father, and in doing so discovers the (loved) self, the identity denied by her father's narcissism. Most importantly, this attachment to Ravenswood is made within her secret life, within the autonomous desires promoted by her fantasies, and while the satiric vocabulary of the novel retains the capacity to place this under fire, the romantic vocabulary persists in confirming its value. Back in the public world, however, Lucy is forced to marry Bucklaw by her mother. The strong mother therefore destroys the secret life and effects a dualistic return of the repressed: she reasserts her domination of her daughter, and in doing so enforces the transference of Lucy's sexual desire to Bucklaw, a weak and well-meaning figure like her father who offers love of an essentially narcissistic kind. In Freudian terms this is a regression in which the mother's reassertion of her dominance is a re-enactment of the pre-Oedipal phase of Lucy's sexuality: she now guides Lucy back from her discovery of the lover as a desired sexual object, to the phase where the mother's dominance gives way to the attachment of the father, here represented by Bucklaw (the text setting up a form of parity between the two figures in terms of their characters). Effectively, then, the mother sanctions the incestuous desire, but Lucy, reacting against the regression, takes revenge upon the weak father-figure. At precisely the moment she is meant to receive him (the wedding night) she wounds him almost fatally. The denial of Lucy's completion through the sexual act is equally a denial of the father-figure's sexual power, a regression to the period of sexual development wherein desire attaches itself to a member of the opposite sex. Within this model, Lucy is sexually incomplete, and this is mirrored by the fragmentary life of madness within which she loses the power of communication and speech. In such a reading, her actions are the result of her ungoverned neuroses.

It is precisely this that presents us with a problem. Within the signifying systems that grant the woman wholeness, identity and sanity through the act of conjugation, Lucy's madness can only represent her incompletion and denote her weakness. In a Freudian diagnosis her neuroses make her particularly vulnerable, and those neuroses are seen as the product of excessive secret desire, or the refusal to enter into marriage. The analysis implicit in Scott's fiction is similar, and confirmed by the tragic language of the novel, set on offering up Lucy's mania as the consequence of her being denied her lover. Yet we need not operate within these constraints, for the Freudian model may be deployed and then disrupted to produce a second reading. Lucy's refusal to concede to her mother's re-making of her sexual development may be seen as a meaningful rebellion and not as a failure to pass from one phase to another. The denial of the father substitute's power can now be seen as a victory over it, an attempt therefore to preserve the secret life wherein desire played only – but successfully – within the precincts of fantasy. In stabbing Bucklaw, therefore, Lucy restores the identity of selfhood that may even have been lost to Ravenswood, for so long as he belongs to that clandestine world, his dominance allows him the opportunity to co-opt it. In stabbing Bucklaw in an act of ritual wounding or castration, Lucy refuses the phallocentric symbolic order. She moves not into the insanity betokening abnormality or arrested development, but into the madness that is the refusal to enter into patriarchal normality, the symbolic order of things that demands her completion within conjugation. Further, she moves beyond the language of such an order. After her cry on discovery ('So, you have ta'en up your bonny bridegroom?') she speaks no more, and will make no explanation – 'convulsion followed convulsion, till they closed in death, without her being able to utter a word explanatory of the fatal scene' (p. 304).

The superimposition of a Freudian model onto the nexus of relationships in which the woman's madness is placed provides two readings. The first projects an available construct into a text whose structures of human relations offer it ready support, but the coincidence here is not accidental. It is to be explained by the fact that Freud and Scott are working within an identifiable tradition of writing which will represent the woman's completion in terms of her conjunction with the man. Any deflection out of this course of things becomes a problem. For Scott, it leads to the creation of an uncertain kind of romantic tragedy, wherein the internal history of the heroine or that which is not open to the other characters in the novel is constantly working against the tragic emotional *dénouement*. For Lucy's history is rendered in terms and figures gleaned from the traditions of eighteenth-century satire, and this satiric vocabulary tends to undermine the romantic plot in its restless desire to criticise the woman, to see her as inconstant, foolish and fanciful:

> the effect, which the various recollections connected with a scene so terrific made upon a mind which was susceptible in an extreme degree, was more permanent than the injury which her nerves had sustained. Visions of terror, both in sleep and in waking reveries, recalled to her the form of the furious animal, and the dreadful bellow with which he accompanied his career; and it was always the image of the Master of Ravenswood, with his native nobleness of countenance and form, that seemed to interpose betwixt her and assured death. It is, perhaps, at all times dangerous for a young person to suffer recollection to dwell repeatedly, and with too much complacency, on the same individual; but in Lucy's situation it was almost unavoidable. She had never happened to see a young man of mien and features so romantic . . . Lucy Ashton, in short, was involved in those mazes of the imagination which are most dangerous to the young and the sensitive. Time, it is true, absence, change of scene and new faces, might probably have destroyed the illusion in her instance, as it has done in many others; but her residence remained solitary, and her mind without those means of dissipating her pleasing visions. (pp. 47–8)

This quasi-satirical dimension of the novel is essentially part of the narrator's knowledge which suffuses the text in the form of a worldly-wise commentary on its actions. The reader is required to defer to this sagacity, and within the moral scheme it proposes, Lucy's selfhood, her solitariness, is regarded as equivalent to a misguided education. When she is alone, her fantasies and desired are 'dangerous', and the resultant instability of mind and character may therefore be finally read as a preconditional factor in her madness. Again then, the isolated woman is presented as unnatural. The novel's narrative knows better than she, for it continually alludes to what it takes to be the eternal truth of woman's need for guidance, the impossibility of her being herself alone. Yet this narrative is partially in opposition to the procedure of the romantic plot which uses Lucy's madness as a means of repressing the satirical element to confirm the tragic. It is a hyperbolic device, therefore, but also a device that is capable of reconciling the novel's paradox and contradictions, for it confirms the woman's subordination which both vocabularies (satiric and romantic) struggle to present. Madness is the result of a deviation from normality – the loss of the man. Further, it proceeds from what Freud would diagnose as a trauma or neurosis, the refusal to transfer the love for the father to his surrogate. In a broad sense, Scott's use of madness is analogous to Freud's identification of the root causes of hysteria. The ideological history in which the work of both writers is enclosed is in this sense remarkably static, for its symbolic order remains unchanged, and has no way of accommodating the woman's whole presence without the sanctification of phallic power.

Yet I hope I have shown through the second reading offered that it is possible to generate a different set of meanings in the text's denouement, an interpretation that takes the otherness of mania as a refusal to defer to the symbolic order rather than as simple abnormality. Here madness may not be placed in antithetical relation to the reason of the status quo, and it becomes instead a means of exposing its fallacies. It is possible to produce this meaning not only on the basis of a set of flexible or volatile terms, but because the text asserts its hierarchical arrangements uncertainly. Within this instability, the romantic plot may be retrieved as a plot of positive action, and Lucy's madness may be seen as an emergent form of integrity. The spilling-over of her secret world into the public domain results in her one autonomous action.

The contest between the romantic and satiric or moral idioms in Scott's novel is a common feature of Gothic texts and many which show the mark of their influence. Here the frisson of horror or romance is freely indulged as an incitement for the reader but rarely allowed to be declared as the *raison d'être* for the work itself. As a consequence, such novels frequently hurry into moral conclusions which sort oddly with their characteristic idiom. *The Monk*, perhaps, is the classic example. *Wuthering Heights*, like *The Bridge of Lammermoor*, may show the traces of this simple opposition, yet in each case it is much subdued and metamorphosed by a new complexity of social relationships. In *Wuthering Heights* it may be seen in the clash of interests between the first half of the novel and the second, this latter being intent upon establishing the humanitarian values threatened by Cathy and Heathcliff. Once again we find the myth of the woman's derangement caught up in this contest of styles, and as in *The Bride of Lammermoor* and *Sense and Sensibility*, much depends on the interpretation of the actual scene in which this derangement is dramatically presented, and its precedents and antecedents, for the whole complex may confirm or subvert either of the novel's oppositional languages.

I am referring to the scenes at the centre of the novel, wherein Heathcliff's return and his confrontation with Edgar Linton engender Cathy's illness. There is no doubt that this illness is first represented as her strategy for avoiding the company of her husband ('And, Nelly, say to Edgar, if you see him again tonight, that I'm in danger of being seriously ill – I wish it may prove true. He has startled and distressed me shockingly! I want to frighten him')[5] and yet equally, it is also beyond question that the illness which evolves is closely linked to the 'excess' of passion and initially, to the symptoms of hysteria:

It was enough to try the temper of a saint, such senseless, wicked rages! There she lay dashing her head against the arm of the sofa, and grinding her teeth, so that you might fancy she would crash them to splinters!

Mr Linton stood looking at her in sudden compunction and fear. He told me to fetch some water. She had no breath for speaking.

I brought a glass full; and, as she would not drink, I sprinkled it on her face. In a few seconds she stretched herself out stiff, and turned up her eyes, while her cheeks, at once blanched and livid assumed the aspect of death.

Linton looked terrified.

'There is nothing in the world the matter,' I whispered. I did not want him to yield, though I could not help being afraid in my heart.

'She has blood on her lips!' he said, shuddering.

'Never mind!' I answered, tartly. And I told him how she had resolved, previous to his coming on, exhibiting a fit of frenzy.

I incautiously gave the account aloud, and she heard me, for she started up – her hair flying over her shoulders, her eyes flashing, the muscles of her neck and arms standing out preternaturally. (pp. 156–7)

At the very onset of Catherine's illness, therefore, the reader is presented with an interpretative difficulty, and its opposing elements are held in suspension by the unreliable participants and commentators on the action, Edgar Linton and Nelly Dean. Nelly, privy like us to Cathy's earlier proclamation, is convinced that she is witnessing a piece of acting, a self-induced frenzy. Edgar, however, stands appalled and frightened by what he sees. Is the woman's illness a mere façade or a genuine mark of her distress? Does it signify weakness in difficult circumstances or the strength of her rebellion? Alternatively, is it self-willed, and therefore within the judgements decreed by common notions of social protocol, a piece of irresponsibility? It is no coincidence that some of these questions and others of a related kind are to be found surrounding the debates about hysteria and related forms of derangement in the nineteenth century – indeed they are the questions that gave birth to the science of psychoanalysis and its new geometry of the relation of body and mind, and its capacity to make such questions largely superogatory. Psychoanalysis notwithstanding, it would be naive to suppose that such questions were purely a matter of history. *Wuthering Heights* sets up the arena in which these time-honoured and politically volatile questions about woman's illness may again enter into dispute with one another, and as in *The Bride of Lammermoor* (and perhaps to a lesser extent, *Sense and Sensibility*) the text finds itself unable to be unequivocal in its judgements.

Ironically enough, it is at this point in the novel that Edgar comments on Cathy's 'insanity' (p. 157), applying the term pejoratively to her insistence on fostering a relationship with Heathcliff. Insanity is not so far away however, and within the terms of early nineteenth century medical diagnosis, Cathy's ensuing 'brain-fever' (as the text calls it) could have been conceived as a form of madness. The novel does not declare Cathy to be mad, but it denotes her condition by way of a classic scene of delirium which is concerned to present the woman denied her lover as a person falling apart. Yet again, feminine derangement is discovered in a drama replete with the symbols of decomposition and fragmentation, as Catherine plucks the feathers from her torn pillow:

> she seemed to find childish diversion in pulling the feathers from the rents she had just made, and ranging them on the sheet according to their different species: her mind had strayed to other associations.
>
> 'That's a turkey's,' she murmured to herself; 'and this is a wild duck's; and this is a pigeon's. Ah, they put pigeons' feathers in the pillows – no wonder I couldn't die! Let me take care to throw it on the floor when I lie down. And here's a moorcock's; and this – I should know it among a thousand – it's a lapwing's. Bonny bird; wheeling over our heads in the middle of the moor. It wanted to get to its nest, for the clouds touched the swells, and it felt rain coming. This feather was picked up from the heath, the bird was not shot – we saw its nest in the winter, full of little skeletons. Heathcliff set a trap over it, and the old ones dare not come. I made him promise he'd never shoot a lapwing after that, and he didn't. Yes, here are more! Did he shoot my lapwings, Nelly? Are they red, any of them? Let me look.' (p. 160)

Like *Sense and Sensibility*, *Wuthering Heights* renders the scenes of the woman's suffering in a highly serious way. The scenes at the centre of the novel have disquieted some readers, who dispose of them by recourse to a pattern of judgement which calls freely on concepts of melodrama and vulgarity. If, on the other hand, the reader is prepared to grant power and weight to this section of the text, it is possible to recognize therein a positive disruption of one code in which the myth of the deranged woman is commonly written. Here she may no longer stand as the repository of feebleness or as the consequence of weak-willed habits. On the contrary, her disjointed outbursts constitute the device by which her independent desire is asserted: 'I wish I could hold you . . . till we were both dead! I shouldn't care what you suffered. I care nothing for your sufferings. Why shouldn't you suffer? I do!' (p. 195). Catherine's selfishness is a denial of her role as reciprocating subservient partner as much as it is an inversion of the Christian code of selfless love. She tears our Heathcliff's hair (p. 195) in an action that traditionally denotes the woman's mutilation of the man's strength; she begs forgiveness for her own sake (p. 196); and through a process of introjection denies her dependence on her lover's body: 'Well, never mind! That is not my Heathcliff. I shall love mine yet; and take him with me – he's in my soul. And . . . the thing that irks me most is this shattered prison after all' (p. 196).

Yet to resolve the questions posed by the text into this one disruptive reading requires the suspension of the narrative so that it may be arrested at this point. Alternatively, the linear development of the plot can be denied in the cause of a reading which takes Cathy's utterances here as the peak of her achievement. If neither of these reading strategies is adopted, the significance of the scene's conclusion will be acknowledged, and here Heathcliff is seen to possess Cathy as he 'gathered her to him with greedy jealousy' (p. 197). In a sharp deviation of that narrative, the power of masculine desire is asserted against the frailty of the woman, here emblematized in Cathy's fainting fit from which she never recovers, her last utterance imploring Heathcliff not to leave – 'I shall die! I shall die!' (p. 199).

Cathy's derangement and death, therefore, are ultimately implicated in the narrative process which reaffirms the culturally determined place of the woman, but that reaffirmation itself is uncomfortably achieved, following so closely after the sequence which describes the assertion of Catherine's power. Here, then, is a fracture in the text which may allow for a rearrangement of its hierarchies in an act of reading prepared to deconstruct the apparent logic of the narrative sequence. Even so, the reader is still left with the root cause of Cathy's derangement, for this, her separation from her lover, would seem to imply a significant kind of dependence, and as such it may be read as a symbolic articulation of a complementary role. But of course, she does not necessarily recognize Heathcliff as her lover, and this hiatus in her knowledge, and indeed in the text itself, allows the intervention of a psychoanalytic reading. Such a reading may explain Cathy's dependence on Heathcliff in terms of the more general confusion or lack of awareness which afflicts her, and given that her disturbance is of a kind that releases symptoms likely to be interpreted as hysterical, this reading may not be considered inappropriate.

The trauma at the centre of the novel may be read in terms of Freud's return of the repressed, though to employ such an approach is hardly new. Catherine's incestuous (or to be literal, quasi-incestuous) love for Heathcliff is repressed to enable her socialized entry into the world of Thrushcross Grange. This passage is accomplished in Heathcliff's absence, so that his return reawakens the incestuous desire and the resultant breakdown, directly engendered by Edgar's impossible proposition:

> To get rid of me – answer my question . . . You must answer it; and that violence does not alarm me. I have found that you can be as stoical as anyone, when you please. Will you give up Heathcliff hereafter, or will you give up me? It is impossible for you to be *my* friend and *his* at the same time; and I absolutely *require* to know which you choose. (p. 156)

In the terms of psychoanalysis Cathy is here faced with a choice either of regression to the phase of incestuous desire, or of reproducing the process of repression. Edgar would make a poor analyst, for he will not allow Cathy consciously to reconcile herself to her love for Heathcliff in the context of her idealized love for him. Freud describes the source of the anxiety:

> Girls with an exaggerated need for affection and an equally exaggerated horror of the real demands made by sexual life have an irresistible temptation on the one hand to realise the ideal of assexual love in their lives and on the other hand to conceal their libido behind an affection which they can express without self-reproaches, by holding fast throughout their lives to their infantile fondness, revived at puberty, for their parents or brothers and sisters. Psychoanalysis has no difficulty in showing persons of this kind that they are *in love*, in the everyday sense of the word, with these blood-relations of theirs; for, with the help of their symptoms and other manifestations of their illness, it traces their unconscious thoughts and translates them into conscious ones.[6]

The abreaction Freud describes cannot take place, for the choice Edgar offers Cathy denies her the ability to complete such an analysis. Accordingly, she breaks down, and this degeneration need not be taken as the congenital condition of a 'weaker sex', but as a condition brought about by her repressive circumstances, and the complexity of her social and sexual relations.

The choice of readings thrown up by *Wuthering Heights* is typical of those encountered in this study. Cathy's delirium and degeneration may be seen as yet another manifestation of a pervasive and deeply-rooted mythology of womankind, weak, unstable, fundamentally incomplete without the man. In such a reading the text remains caught in the dominant ideology. Yet the romantic plot of the novel (also an essential historical feature of its production) acts as a powerful and subversive agent working against what may be seen as the text's wider moral concerns, the reconciliation of the two worlds it presents in the social development of the second Catherine and her marriage to Hareton. In this action it develops Cathy as a figure struggling for self-determination, unwilling to settle for what she is offered by either of her lovers. This is most clearly seen in the almost manic scenes of her delirium and the frenzied confrontation with Heathcliff, and at these moments she allows the reader to disrupt the economy of difference and sexual relations that informs the rest of the text. In the three novels discussed so far in this chapter, closely related structures are seen to be at work, although they have different effects. In each case two idioms or modes dispute with one another, and within this conflict the woman's illness plays a crucial role, enabling the reader to break the web of meaning spun by the novel's broad moral concerns, a web strung around the dominant ideology, or alternatively, to trace just how secure are its points of suspension even under stress. It is perhaps only the Romantic novel, with its awkward handling of the woman's sensibility, that compounds this curious yet rich chemistry.

These truly Romantic women, emerging unabashed from the concerns of an age of sensibility, find a strange successor in Miss Havisham in Dickens' *Great Expectations*. In one sense, Miss Havisham is clearly deranged, yet the derangement is not indicated so much by her utterances as the ritual of her daily life, her paraphernalia, and her wasting physical form. The text gratefully receives the myth of the deserted woman and effects an odd displacement by projecting her decomposition onto the items of furniture with which she is surrounded, onto her half-dressed state (that of the incomplete bride) and of course, onto her body:

> I saw that the bride within the bridal dress had withered like the dress, and like the flowers, and had no brightness left but the brightness of her sunken eyes. I saw that the dress had been put upon the rounded figure of a young woman, and that the figure upon which it now hung loose, had shrunk to skin and bone. Once I had been taken to see some ghastly waxwork at the Fair, representing I know not what impossible personage lying in state. Once I had been taken to one of our old marsh churches to see a skeleton in the ashes of a rich dress, that had been dug out of a vault under the church pavement. Now, waxwork and skeleton seemed to have dark eyes that moved and looked at me.[7]

Miss Havisham is put on show by the novel, and a new vocabulary for the depiction of the deranged and deserted woman is here emerging, deriving perhaps from the Victorian circus or sideshow. Pip sees her as a freak, the reified object of a financial enterprise, and there is irony here, for it is Pip who is the paid entertainer. This freakishness of Miss Havisham's is consistently played upon in the novel, and the result is that she comes before the reader as a monstrous parody of the nullified afterlife assumed to be the lot of the woman deserted at the alter. The marriage ceremony is here the undeclared master-code denoting completion, and the denial of that wholeness is continually alluded to in the symbolically constructed interior of Satis House. Yet *Great Expectations* is also vitally concerned with the language of the body: Miss Havisham denotes her fragmentation by the grandiloquent and touching gesture that uses her body as the index to her emotional life ('What do I touch?' 'Your heart.' 'Broken!' (p. 88)) even while her mind – despite what she calls her 'sick fancies' – is always seen through Pip's understanding as intact.

For Pip, this early scene is a moment of great consequence. He enters Satis House as an incompetent reader, interpolated between us and a real text somewhere beyond our direct apprehension. He is unable to see the full significance of the arrested clocks, the wedding-gown, the jewellery and Estella, and the lacuna in his knowledge is a clear indication of what the reader must seek to find. To Pip, Miss Haversham is sane, yet her body is incomplete: her broken heart has a literal meaning for him, forged by the association with his own fear of mutilation first felt in his initial encounter with Magwitch, whose imaginary friend, the young man, has 'a secret way pecooliar to himself of getting at a boy, and at his heart, and at his liver' (p. 38). When Miss Havisham touches her heart, Pip is reminded of the young man, whose threat of mutilation is now passed on into the person of Estella, encouraged to play cards with Pip so that she may 'break his heart' (p. 89). Here an important transformation is effected, in that Pip's fear for his body is revived in an encounter that is essentially sexual. Miss Havisham's 'sick fancy' is to see the male mutilated, and the game of cards, accordingly, only leads to his utter humiliation and proven impotence as a young lover. So Pip's emergent power as an adolescent is emasculated first by Magwitch (powerful father surrogate) and then by Miss

Havisham (in whom he insistently recognizes a fairy-godmother) through Estella, the progeny of the father, the male witch, and the foster-child of the mother, the female witch.

Great Expectations therefore places the familiar figure of the deserted and deranged woman in a position of unfamiliar power in terms of her influence over the novel's actions and characters. At the same time, that control is being constantly limited and qualified. In its insistent avoidance of 'normal' family structures, the text constructs two apparently distinct spheres of influence which may be termed matriarchal and patriarchal, the first dominated by Mrs Gargery and Miss Havisham, the second by Jaggers and Magwitch on his return. In turn, this division in the text effects the disposition of the elements of its matriarchal sphere into types: Miss Havisham, deranged in her person and possessions yet apparently sane in mind, who wishes to cripple Pip's emotional life; Mrs Gargery, who mutilates Pip's body and loses her mind in Orlick's assault. Yet these apparently powerful women only exert their influence over their houses, Mrs Gargery by her rampaging cleaning of her surroundings, Miss Havisham by her wilful neglect of hers. Moreover, the 'patriarchal' control which Jaggers exerts so overtly in the second half of the novel is tacitly present in the first, where feminine power, it turns out, is uncertainly asserted. For here Joe is established as a moral centre whose force accumulates in the course of the novel, and more significantly, Mrs Gargery's domination, constantly subject to Pumblechook's approval, is seen to be ultimately vulnerable to the act of masculine violence which destroys her. These feminine types and their influence therefore deserve further scrutiny, and in particular, the relation between the deranged and the imbecile matriarchs, Miss Havisham and Mrs Gargery, demands the attention of this study.

If Biddy is the closest the novel comes to the ideal woman according to its own moral formulae, then Miss Havisham and Mrs Gargery, the dominant mothers, are depicted against her rectitude. Pip as incompetent reader cannot initially recognize this, for he mistakenly takes Biddy for a lover and not a guardian. The text's intention is clearly to enthrone Biddy at the centre of its moral enterprise, to praise her patience, tolerance and quiet acceptance of circumstances, and in order to do this it exploits myths of woman's madness in new and possibly unique ways. Thus while the novel takes Biddy as Pip's most proper mother, it exaggerates his errors in identifying Miss Havisham and even his sister as mothers by presenting them as figures of the deranged mind. Mrs Gargery's derangement is initially less obvious than Miss Havisham's, and may be regarded as a species of the eccentricity which attends so many of Dickens' characters, but it is evident in her rampaging, and particularly in her bizarre display designed to goad Joe into fighting Orlick:

> 'To hear the names he's giving me! That Orlick! In my own house! Me, a married woman! With my husband standing by! O! O!' Here my sister, after a fit of clappings and screamings, beat her hands upon her bosom and upon her knees, and threw her cap off, and pulled her hair down – which were the last stages on her road to frenzy. Being by this time a perfect Fury and a complete success, she made a dash at the door, which I had fortunately locked. (p. 142)

Here we are back to self-induced frenzy according to Pip's narrative, which also insists upon diagnosing it as a specifically feminine ploy, there being no excuse for woman's violence: 'I must remark of my sister, what is equally true of all the violent women I have ever seen, that passion was no excuse for her, because it is undeniable that instead of lapsing into passion, she consciously and deliberately took extraordinary pains to force herself into it' (p. 142). Nevertheless, Mrs Gargery's loss of self is finally developed into imbecility after Orlick's attack. This derangement is to be sharply distinguished from the more common usage of the madwoman myth in fiction, which as I have shown is most commonly implicated for the purposes of confirming the tragedy of the woman alone after desertion. For Mrs Gargery's loss of mind is punitive, confirmed as such by the manner of her presentation after the attack, wherein she becomes more like Biddy in her exhibitions of patience, forgiveness and kindness. She moves closer to the novel's moral centre, and her imbecility, oddly correspondent to the derangement of the Romantic woman, is thus a means of rendering her more 'normal' rather than indicating the absence of normality (the conjoined existence) as in most earlier uses of the device.

This is a sinister shift of some consequence. *Great Expectations* scrambles the components of woman's mythical madness to produce new arrangements and emphases, a new symbolic structure which moves around concepts of eccentric sado-masochism (Miss Havisham) and imbecility (Mrs Gargery) rather than the sentimental motif of derangement following loss. While the traces of the earlier myth may be seen in Miss Havisham's desertion at the altar, the loss of mind or faculties is displaced onto Mrs Gargery, who is implicated in a different arrangement, perhaps an anti-romantic arrangement, which initially grants her matriarchal and phallic power (asserted via Tickler) only to divest her of that power by way of a violent phallic attack. The ultimate consequence of this attack is her silencing, her transformation into the mute object bearing only subdued indications of comprehension. Only at this point may she be regarded as anything like the sentimentalized romantic woman, and even then her tragedy is overshadowed by her humility and the crude moral message which it serves. In this arrangement of Mrs Gargery's history, Orlick occupies the central position. He is the hammer (the hieroglyph she chooses for him) that silences and normalizes the woman. The text is at pains to illustrate her gratitude, for it becomes her habit to have Orlick come and stand before her daily, after having shown 'every possible desire to conciliate him' (p. 151). Orlick sees himself as being the man that will give Mrs Gargery what her husband will not provide: 'Ah-h-h . . . I'd hold you if you was my wife. I'd hold you under the pump, and choke it out of you' (p. 142), and after completing the deed he sings – oddly to Pip's mind – the song of phallic power 'Old Clem' ('Beat it out, beat it out – Old Clem!') the song which soothes Miss Havisham as Pip and Jaggers push her round and round the room in a bizarre parody of the symbolism of sexual completion.

Orlick has been seen as Pip's alter-ego, and certainly Pip's implication in the attack on his sister is very full.[8] 'I was at first disposed to believe that *I* must have had some hand in the attack upon my sister,' he remarks; and even when considering the matter in what he feels to be a more reasonable light, he is troubled by the thought that he had provided the weapon (p. 148). This identification of the two characters might open the way for a discussion on the possibility of the subdued presence of incestuous desire in the text, but I am more interested in the way in which the Pip–Orlick relation reinforces the Mrs Joe–Miss Havisham identification at which I have previously hinted. Thus, when Mrs Gargery, supine and broken, has Orlick placed before her, needing his forgiveness, the scene is paralleled much later in the novel when Pip goes to Satis House to receive Miss Havisham's money for Herbert, and she falls on her knees before him begging forgiveness. In both instances the women are normalized, temporarily retrieved from derangement or imbecility, as they are pulled into a position of childish dependence. Miss Havisham kneels with her folded hands held up to Pip 'in the manner in which, when her poor heart was young and fresh and whole, they must have been raised to heaven from her mother's side' (p. 410), while Mrs Gargery watches Orlick 'as if she were particularly wishful to be answered that he took kindly to his reception'. Further, 'there was an air of humble propitiation in all she did, such as I have seen pervade the bearing of a child towards a hard master' (p. 151). And just as both women, in their moments of resolution become childlike, so too they become providers: Mrs Gargery wishes to give Orlick something to drink, and Miss Havisham provides for Herbert, and more significantly, expresses a wish to provide for Pip. In both scenes the women are reconstituted as mothers, retrieved from their realms of abnormality to become good little women, and the reconstitution occurs through Pip's vision of them as children. His process of growth and gaining of power through knowledge is achieved alongside an apparent regression in the lives of the women who have dominated him.

The woman's derangement – if I may use the term to refer simultaneously to Miss Havisham's disturbed state and Mrs

Gargery's physical disabilities – is therefore of great symbolic consequence in the novel. It becomes the passage through which they are routed towards the kind of morality represented by Biddy, and in both cases it is punitive, a penance of a kind which they must serve in order to discover what Dickens (wittingly or otherwise) suggests is the proper condition of womankind. In Miss Havisham's case this penance is self-inflicted, but Mrs Gargery's is administered by the growing power of the male world. Both women begin the novel as fantastic embodiments of weird power: Mrs Gargery with her pins and Tickler, marking the body under her control by beatings and her pushing of Pip against the wall so that its paint is transferred to his forehead; Miss Havisham with her stick and her perverse demands, mutilating the minds under her control. Both are sources of *maleficium*, and *Great Expectations* carried the deranged woman back to her seventeenth-century predecessor, the witch. And both, like Magwitch – the master-witch – are brought to book by the text's moral concerns, made to recant before being killed off.

The knowledge held by Miss Havisham and Mrs Gargery is never a major part of the novel's concerns, and the events leading to their afflictions, though known or deduced, are not narrated. Their half-told or implied stories are seemingly only of remote interest within the wider machinery of the text which is so evidently intent on obscuring its women's histories, so that they become figures of mystery and mystification. Nowhere is this more obvious than in the case of Molly, Estella's mother, whose story is contained within the massive repressive power of male knowledge, exemplified in the scene at Jaggers' dinner party:[9]

'If you talk of strength', said Mr Jaggers, '*I'll* show you a wrist. Molly, let them see your wrist.' Her entrapped hand was on the table, but she had already put her other hand behind her waist. 'Master,' she said, in a low voice, with her eyes attentively and entreatingly fixed upon him. 'Don't.'

Jaggers' idiosyncratic and cryptic bragging is simultaneously a means of sharing his power with the young men around his table, and Pip, the initiate, here finds the beginnings of the knowledge that will eventually allow him full self-governance. Jaggers knows Molly's story, and the evidence which will lead to its discovery is imprinted on her body. The stories of Miss Havisham and Mrs Gargery, like their full names, will only be half-known, and the details are written not so much on the body (we know nothing of Mrs Joe's scars) but in their deranged and silenced minds.

In the case of Mrs Gargery, there is perhaps not so very much to learn. We know she was attacked, and she seemingly knows her attacker, but her story is eventually told only by Orlick when he captures Pip, and then briefly. The case of Miss Havisham is very different. 'If you knew all my story,' she says to Pip, 'you would have some compassion for me, and a better understanding of me' (p. 412). Pip replies that he does know the story, and that it has inspired him 'with great commiseration'. He hopes he understands it. But Pip has always mistaken knowledge for understanding: like Jaggers (a true father to him in this respect) it is seemingly all he needs to progress towards the acquisition of power. But Pip's acquiring of this knowledge, however much he has pondered it, is in fact very oblique, for it comes to him from Herbert in broken pieces, interspersed by lessons on table-manners. The relation between the discourse on table-manners and the history of Miss Havisham however is not arbitrary, for both are sermons on how to behave as a gentleman (much is made of Miss Havisham's gentlemanly father and the gentlemanly pretensions of her suitor) and so when Pip asks, at its termination, 'is that all the story?' (p. 205) the answer must be no, and the negative recalled when Miss Havisham pleads the significance of *all* her story in the final scene at Satis House.

In each of the texts I have considered in this chapter the woman's derangement is in some way contiguous to her silence, her inability to tell her own story or the repression which will not allow her to articulate her feelings or desires. Consequently, she is spoken for, mediated and often corrected, by the dominant centres – moral and political – in each case, and her story, like her condition, is inevitably fragmentary and forever incomplete. Within these centres of power, the letter or written document plays a crucial role, both in excluding the women and in allowing them some intermittent contact. It is the written marriage contract which leads directly to Lucy Ashton's madness; it is Willoughby's letter which engenders Marianne's disturbance; the final climax of frenzy in *Wuthering Heights* is preceded by Heathcliff's note to Cathy. Yet it is in *Great Expectations* – perhaps not surprisingly given its concern with law and evidence – that the written word carries the most powerful authenticity, and is therefore to be found playing a major role. Miss Havisham's desertion at the altar was apparently marked by her reception of a letter from her betrothed, and she sees her way back into some kind of reconciliation with the male world through the powers of the written word:

> I took the tablets from her hand, and it trembled again, and it trembled more as she took off the chain to which the pencil was attached and put it in mine. All this she did without looking at me.
>   'My name is on the first leaf. If you can ever write under my name "I forgive her," though ever so long after my broken heart is dust – pray do it!' (p. 410)

Likewise Mrs Gargery attempts to drag herself back from the isolation of her state through the use of the slate, and much play is made of the errors of interpretation and signification that ensue. Just as Pip (in a sense) can restore Miss Havisham through writing, so Biddy completes the 'mysterious sign' inscribed by Pip's sister on the slate, by seeing the hammer as Orlick. This is not a matter of naming but of signifying – 'she had lost his name and could only signify him by his hammer' (p. 151). Biddy thus restores Mrs Gargery temporarily back into contact with the world of normal communication through her interpretation of the inscription, and yet the function of this is to secure her a subservient role beneath Orlick's phallic violence. In this sense her partial mastery of a code is a form of deference to the order of things which relegates her. While Mrs Gargery struggles to signify in her disablement, her erstwhile repressed husband learns to write. Mrs Gargery cannot write properly, and therefore, in a very broad and odd respect, she is analogous to Marianne in *Sense and Sensibility*, who is rebuked by a horrified Elinor for her 'improper' writing to Willoughby. The woman's entry into the most dominant and authentic social code is therefore uncertain and fraught with difficulties.

A similar uncertainty can be seen in *The Bride of Lammermoor*, when Lucy, having signed the document betrothing her to Bucklaw with 'slight tremulous irregularity', subsequently removes the broken ring from her neck at Ravenswood's request (pp. 286–7). Here writing supersedes symbol in the contest for power. Although Ravenswood falters momentarily ('And she could wear it thus . . . could wear it in her very bosom – could wear it next to her heart – even when') his moment of doubt is exorcised by his vehement trust in the newly written document, and significantly, he throws the ring into the fireplace, which is where Lucy is discovered in her insanity, searching perhaps for the remnants of the code which gave her meaning. Mrs Gargery with her ideographic inscriptions, Marianne with her improper letters, Lucy with her broken ring, even Miss Havisham with the language of Satis House, all subscribe to their own codes which threaten the dominant systems of communication and speak for the urgency of their own desires. But these alternative codes are finally supressed or taken over by the invasion of the written document, the tyranny of the sane and stable letter over the eccentric peculiarity of the woman's symbolic language, through which she may live her secret life.

While the plots of these novels will attempt to suppress these alternative codes or take them over through the powers of the written document, thus asserting the tyranny of the sane and stable letter over the eccentric peculiarity of the woman's symbolic language, the invasion of the woman's madness by such means is always awkward and never complete. In Irigaray's words, one must listen differently, for the 'other meaning' here in the woman's refusal of the letter, is the embracing of her own words and the casting off of others 'to avoid becoming fixed, immobilized.'

Notes

1. Elaine Marks and Isabelle de Courtivron, *New French Feminisms* (Brighton, 1981), p. 103.
2. Jane Austen, *Sense and Sensibility*, edited by Tony Tanner (Harmondsworth, 1969), p. 195. All references and quotations are from this edition, and page references follow in parentheses.
   Francis Danby's painting is dated 1821, and is to be found in the Victoria and Albert Museum, London. In medical terms 'disappointed love' was synonomous with 'erotomania' and it is therefore possible that the painting's title is directly concerned with trying to suggest something of its subject's state of mind as well as her history. Raymond Lister's brief commentary on the poem does not pick this up, but still suggests the presence of derangement by way of a parallel with Ophelia. See Raymond Lister, *Victorian Narrative Paintings* (London, 1966), p. 42.
3. 'Nervous irritability' was a term widely used in the medical writings of the late eighteenth century, and referred generally to disorders of the nervous system deriving from excessive (and often 'womanly') sensibility. For a gloss and summary, see Michel Foucault, *Madness and Civilization: A History of Insanity in the Age of Reason*, translated by Richard Howard (London, 1971), pp. 154–8.
4. Sir Walter Scott, *The Bride of Lammermoor, The Waverley Novels*, standard edition, 25 vols (London, 1896), VIII, 26. All references and quotations are from this edition, and page numbers follow in parentheses.
5. Emily Brontë, *Wuthering Heights*, edited by David Daiches (Harmondsworth, 1965), p. 155. All references and quotations are from this edition, and page references follow in parentheses.
6. Sigmund Freud, *On Sexuality. Three Essays on the Theory of Sexuality*, translated under the general editorship of James Strachey, edited by Angela Richards, *The Pelican Freud Library* (Harmondsworth, 1977), Vol 7, 151.
7. Charles Dickens, *Great Expectations*, edited by Angus Calder (Harmondsworth, 1965), p. 87. All references and quotations are from this edition, and page numbers follow in parentheses.
8. See for example Harry Stone, *Dickens and the Invisible World: Fairy Tales, Fantasy, and Novel-Making* (London, 1980), pp. 303–9. Stone's argument is a full and illuminating one, and takes in the novel's later identification of Pip and Orlick in the scene where the latter accuses the former of murdering his sister (p. 347).
9. When Pip first sees Molly in this scene, he associates her too with witchcraft, seeing her not as a witch, but as a symbol of witchcraft's knowledge, her face looking 'as if it were all disturbed by fiery air, like the faces [he] had seen rise out of the witches' cauldron' (p. 235). The reference is to *Macbeth*, the faces being those foretelling the sequence of succession to the throne. Like Macbeth, Pip sees the knowledge symbolically represented by the 'apparition'.

CHAPTER FIVE

Different Desires:

Jane Eyre and *Wide Sargasso Sea*

To some, the madwoman in *Jane Eyre* may appear little more than a melodramatic convenience, or perhaps another means by which Charlotte Brontë is able to diminish Rochester's potential criminality as a bigamist. By making Bertha Mason insane, the author excuses his desire for Jane and renders him deserving of pity. The victim of an appalling deception, Rochester's attempt to marry twice is thus not a form of avarice, but a desire born of deprivation. The horrors of his marriage are unimaginable, and his planned life with Jane may be regarded by the reader as a justifiable release. Moreover, Rochester's suffering in his marriage both test and cultivate his heroism: his trials prove him to be above the degradations of cruelty ('I would not use cruelty')[1] and suicide, and the text ensures that he emerges as morally honourable by having him attempt to rescue the frenzied Bertha from the burning roof of Thornfield Hall. Such a reading is straightforward enough. It explains the madwoman's presence as a device enlisted in the cause of Rochester's characterization, and it carries with it the endorsement of the novel's 'radical' morality which sets the individual right of self-determination against the frustrations and impediments of institutions and customs. But as some recent studies have recognized, the figure of Bertha Mason and her madness are of more consequence than this, being of great signficance in the novel's wider symbolic apparatus, and forming part of its obliquely powerful method of defining the relations, and the nature of the ambitions and desires of Jane, Rochester and Bertha herself.[2]

Gil + Goo

It is not part of my purpose to reiterate these arguments which are readily available. Rather, I wish to develop certain of the insights therein in combination with the particular interests of this study. The conventional arrangement of the myth of the woman's madness is that lunacy or derangement succeeds desertion, often at the altar. *Jane Eyre*, rather like *Great Expectations*, effects a rich reorganization of the myth's components by placing a deserted woman, here Jane herself, at the centre of the novel as a repository of its moral concerns (which are, and yet are not, normal) while displacing the woman's madness into an incomplete yet crucially important sub-plot. The deserted woman remains sane, and struggles to find independence in her remaining life, while madness no longer indicates womanly weakness or the impossibility of a life alone. It is used here in new ways: as a means of defining the nature of desire, and as a concomitant to this, as an indicator of the monstrous nature of the woman's sexual appetite. In this later sense it combines the myth of woman's madness with the myth of her ungovernable libido.

On the return of the ill-fated wedding party to Thornfield Hall, Rochester presents the assembled company with a tableau of his own devising:

'That is *my wife*,' said he. 'Such is the sole conjugal embrace I am ever to know – such are the endearments which are to solace my leisure hours! and *this* is what I wished to have' (laying his hand upon my shoulder) 'this young girl, who stands so grave and quiet at the mouth of hell, looking collectedly at the gambols of a demon. I wanted her just as a change after that fierce ragout. Wood and Briggs, look at the difference! Compare these clear eyes with the red balls yonder – this face with that mask – this form with that bulk; then judge me . . . (p. 322)

'I wanted her' – Bertha's madness is not just simply the chaotic opposite to Jane's composure, but the means of defining a crucial difference in Rochester's desires. The bitterly ironic metaphor he employs mobilizes the notion of appetite: Bertha's wild assault, the struggle for power between opposing 'virilities' (p. 321) succeeded by the subjugation and temporary paralysing of Bertha as Rochester ties her to the chair, these are the battles of one appetite against another, in the language of the Kleinians, the struggle of the 'good' object against the 'bad'.[3] The dominant language of the novel asserts Rochester's civilized heroism against Bertha's animalism. In the preceding struggle we read such details as 'he could have settled her with a well-planted blow; but he would not strike: he would only wrestle' (p. 321). Bertha is here the unnatural and monstrous woman who tries to bite Rochester, to mutilate the dominant male, a creature whom Jane is initially unable to distinguish as 'beast or human being' (p. 321). Opposition is anything but true friendship as the unnaturalness of Bertha's lunacy is subjected to the 'natural' control of the husband's strength and ultimate mastery.

Sandra Gilbert and Susan Gubar have shown how Bertha's confinement in the attic of Thornfield Hall is a replication of Jane's confinement in the red room, and in an irresistible argument which sees Bertha as Jane's 'truest and darkest double' they demonstrate how the madwoman acts out Jane's repressed and angry desires – to tear the wedding garments, to oppose Rochester's physical power, even to destroy Thornfield itself. It is true that the identification between Jane and Bertha is very strong. In this central tableau however, Rochester splits the doppelgängers, placing himself between the reflected images as the agent of differentiation. What he wants, the differences of his desires, dictates the reason that the text's rhetoric is intent on reinforcing. He wants Jane's youthful and composed innocence as against Bertha's demonic power, her slight form and her clear eyes against the incensed bulk and glaring expression of his wife. He wants the socialized norm beyond the mirror (for that is what he believes Jane is at this stage in the novel, even if he is dimly aware of her special qualities) and not the pre-socialized image of self obsessed with its own wholeness and power.[5]

Yet Rochester's desires were once very different. Earlier he is attracted to Blanche Ingram because she is 'a strapper – a real strapper, Jane: big, brown, and buxom' (p. 248), and his initial attraction to Bertha, seemingly a consequence of youthful giddiness, is equally a description of the nature of his desire:

I found her a fine woman, in the style of Blanche Ingram: tall, dark, and majestic. . . . She flattered me, and lavishly displayed for my pleasure her charms and accomplishments. All the men in her circle seemed to admire her and envy me. I was dazzled, stimulated: my senses were excited; . . . Her relatives encouraged me: competitors piqued me: she allured me: a marriage was achieved before I knew where I was. (pp. 332–3).

Moreover, in the distinction which the text is determined on making here, which in the terms of its own grammar might be described as the distinction between Rochester's sensual desire (Blanche, Bertha) and his desire for the companionship Jane offers, it seems to resort to the coy suggestion that Rochester's appetite led him into the necessity of marriage. At least, that is one interpretation that might be offered for the rather cryptic remark he makes to Jane in a moment of self-forgetfulness: 'I married her: gross, grovelling, mole-eyed blockhead that I was! With less sin I might have – but let me remember to whom I am speaking' (p. 333). But the most important element in Rochester's account of his marriage and Bertha's 'pygmy intellect and giant propensities' is its establishment of a continuum between the depravity indicated in this phrase and her madness. For Bertha's lunacy is not merely hereditary. In a key moment, Rochester asserts that 'her excesses had prematurely developed the germs of insanity'. As for the nature of these 'excesses' we can be left in no doubt, and can only speculate about their detail, for Rochester has already announced that he found himself 'bound to a wife at once intemperate and unchaste' with 'a nature the most gross, impure, depraved' (p. 334). If Rochester's desire for the woman has in fact been the desire for the woman's desire, then he rapidly tires of this. He sees himself as self-deceived. Having projected his desire onto the woman, he is dismayed at the consequences. He sees her as a monster, wild and depraved. The conventional Byronic hero's intemperance has been displaced onto the object of this appetite, and his sin, so essential to the frisson which he offers the reader, apparently really is a sin when it resides in the woman. As in *Great Expectations*, the romance of the woman's madness has disappeared in a fictional scheme which uses derangement as a punishment for excess of a kind.

The confounding of Bertha's madness with her depravity allows *Jane Eyre* to metamorphose the mad woman into the monster all the more easily, and it makes way too, for the manner of her disposal. Most importantly though, it means that Jane's antithetical delineation against Bertha involves a twofold enforcement: her sanity is control of the mind, independence, reasonableness, but it is also control or absence of overt sexual desire. For a brief moment, in what has been described as the central confrontation of *Jane Eyre*[6] – Bertha's attack on Rochester – the power of female desire is released, as the woman driven mad by her lusts springs upon her husband in an impassioned act of attempted mutilation. Rochester's mastery here is his mastery of the woman's passion, a repression of the 'bad' object (the phallic woman, perhaps) which is replaced by his turning to Jane (the 'good' object) – 'this is what I wish to have'. 'To have' – the verb of possession and desire governs this part of the novel. What Rochester wants is its means of articulating Jane's 'worthiness'. What he doesn't want is Bertha's madness, the mistaken desire of desire, which the novel represents as unworthy.

What is it then that Jane wants? Most readers would agree that her need is to be accepted 'equal – as we are' outside the 'medium of custom, conventionalities . . . mortal flesh' (p. 281) as a kind of disembodied spirit. This desexualizing may lead into some sort of explanation for Rochester's maiming, which is neither merely punitive nor simply a castration. Arguing along similar lines, Sandra Gilbert and Susan Gubar suggest that Rochester and Jane now meet as equal – 'like Jane, he draws his powers from within himself, rather than from inequity, disguise, deception . . . being equals, he and Jane can afford to depend upon each other with no fear of one exploiting the other.'[7] This is a strong reading, supported by the conventional symbolism of the novel and the reclamation of Charlotte Brontë as a feminist writer. But in the characterisation of the relationship with which the novel ends, Bertha still plays a role, and her 'depravity' remains as a means of defining Jane's sanity and chastity.

As Bertha's madness is an extension of her former lapses into 'depraved animalism', so, in curious correspondence,

Rochester's mutilation places him on the edge of bestiality. When Jane first sees him on her return as he steps out into the twilight at Ferndean, she sees what she describes as a change in his countenance. Now 'desperate and brooding', he reminds her of some 'wronged and fettered wild beast or bird, dangerous to approach' (p. 456). Subsequently in her banter Jane announces, 'It is time someone undertook to rehumanize you . . . for I see you are being metamorphosed into a lion, or something of that sort.' He is a Nebuchadnezzar figure, his hair like eagle's feathers (p. 461). While Rochester's conduct in his new condition finds no directly meaningful correlation in Bertha's, he is, nevertheless, like her, a kept creature, uncertainly pacing his confined space. Thus, as Rochester once came to his demonic and animalistic wife to repress and restrain, Jane returns to the bestial Rochester to nurture and coax him back into humanity. The animalism of both is brought on by the excess of desire: in Bertha it results in the premature manifestation of her hereditary madness, while Rochester is symbolically punished for his desire (for Jane) by the maiming that will eventually establish his faith in Providence. At least, that is his own reading.[8] But of course, Jane's therapy, her wish to make Rochester whole again, is a possibility only because it does not meet the impediment of madness. That is reserved for the woman who remains eternally fragmented and confined. Jane's reconstitution of Rochester that enables them to meet as whole people is completed against the unwholesomeness of Bertha's madness, which is at once the unwholesomeness of the woman's desire. Her sexual depravity is unforgiveable whereas Rochester's is not.

It is in this way that the novel finds itself likely to be ensnared by the ideology it attempts to subvert through Jane (with a little help from Providence). Critics such as Sandra Gilbert and Susan Gubar, and Susan Siefert are surely right to reclaim *Jane Eyre* for feminism, reducing the emphasis on such elements as her apparent servility and deference, denying the suspect psycho-biographic readings which take Rochester's 'castration' is indicating authorial anxiety, and stressing alternatively Jane's anger (Gilbert and Gubar) or her self-definition (Siefert).[9] But the valorization of Jane is necessarily accomplished at the expense of Bertha, the former representing the good and the wholesome partner for the man, the latter the bad and decadent. Woman's madness in this novel is an essential antithetical device in a whole complex of mirror or reversed images which are employed as a means of ordering its relationships into coherence. Bertha serves as an opposite to Jane, and as an opposite to Rochester, and in both roles she is pushed into the ideological space already waiting for her as a consequence of Charlotte Brontë's concern to liberate Jane and Rochester from its confines. She is the licentious woman, the powerful figure of desire, condemned into madness by her transgression of gender roles. While Rochester can confess to his libertine youth and sexuality, Bertha's desire is unthinkable and monstrous.⌉

⌈It is precisely this dichotomy, this double standard, which Jean Rhys's *Wide Sargasso Sea* splits apart. In a superbly ironic moment late in the novel, Bertha – here renamed (and significantly reidentified) as Antoinette Cosway – stands before Grace Poole in the attic at Thornfield Hall, holding up her red dress to her body, and says, 'Does it make me look intemperate and unchaste? . . . That man told me so.'[10] 'That man' is Rochester, and the subtle yet very precise allusion to the crucial lines in *Jane Eyre* by which Rochester characterizes the nature of Bertha's madness to Jane effects a peculiar reversal. In *Jane Eyre* it is the voice of sanity or normality which stigmatizes Bertha's derangement as being unworthy of sympathy and therapeutic care: Rochester's disgust at her excess is the text's means of defining Jane's purity and denigrating Bertha's sexuality. In the process, the claim that she is depraved and licentious conveniently disposes of Jane's objection that madness in itself should not be treated punitively. Here the novel's moral organization falls into place around Rochester's judgement, the patriarchal judgement of the double standard. But in *Wide Sargasso Sea*, it is the voice of supposed insanity ('supposed' because the issue is in doubt right up until the final pages) that takes up Rochester's accusation and supplies it with its own history in which the 'excess' of Antoinette/Bertha is established by the rumours which accumulate around her family and her romantic and youthful attachment with Sandi. And thus her plangent murmurs in the confinement of Thornfield attic 'accidentally' evoke the justification at the very centre of *Jane Eyre*'s moral scheme, and in this act of evocation, effect a radical and disruptive reading of the earlier novel.

Jean Rhys has read *Jane Eyre* extremely well. Her novel is so much more than an imaginative exercise or supplement it is a re-writing and a re-reading simultaneously which sets a lever at an almost indiscernible fissure in Charlotte Brontë's text. With a little exploratory prising however, this apparently small fissure opens wide to reveal a predictable pattern: Bertha is the bestial madwoman and permanently condemned as such because she has threatened the sexual code which Rochester's story exemplifies, the code which recognizes his depravity as only a venial sin and therefore remediable. In the social conditions of *Jane Eyre*'s production this matter can be left as deliberately vague, deserving even, of the novelist's casual reference since it is so easily assumed to be part of a well-established (although unjust) moral code and practice. In the social conditions of later readings such as Jean Rhys's however, this vagueness, the dextrous trick by which *Jane Eyre* answers its own awkward questions (Jane's 'she cannot help being mad') offers the purchase by which its assumptions may be clearly exposed and questioned. For Jean Rhys it is a point of departure, and Bertha's/Antoinette's 'does it make me look intemperate and unchaste? . . . That man told me so' takes up what *Jane Eyre* seemingly takes as a factual history, and re-casts it as a false accusation. Antoinette's musing over this accusation is a most powerful moment in the novel for another reason, one closely related to this issue of the double standard and the woman's desire. In holding up the dress she is effectively recalling the nature of Rochester's desire in *Wide Sargasso Sea*, a fetishistic obsession which takes as its object Antoinette's dresses, and in particular, one dress. By way of the narrative structure which allows Rochester and Antoinette to tell their own stories, we are left in no doubt that this desire is Rochester's and not a part of Antoinette's imagination, for it is described in his narrative, almost in the form of a confession:

[One afternoon the sight of a dress which she'd left lying on her bedroom floor made me breathless and savage with desire. When I was exhausted I turned away from her and slept, still without a word or a caress. I woke and she was kissing me – soft, light kisses. 'It is late,' she said and smiled. 'You must let me cover you up – the land breeze can be cold.' (p. 78)]

[Antoinette subsequently asks if she should wear the dress Rochester likes, and if he would be pleased if she made another like it, and the reply is affirmative. When she holds up the dress before Grace Poole, therefore, and recalls Rochester's accusation that it made her look intemperate and unchaste, she combines his earlier desire with his later rejection: the once 'good' object is now the 'bad', and the suggestion that the look of intemperance and unchasteness was once precisely what Rochester wanted, is strong. As I have indicated in the discussion above, the germ of this idea is subtly but potently presented in *Jane Eyre*.]

[Jean Rhys is singular if not unique in giving the madwoman a voice, for it is a rare privilege, breaking up the conventional mythology which maintains the strange otherness of insanity by silencing its utterances or permitting them only as fragments, intrusions in the logic and sequence which is the progress of the text, or the consistency of the narrator's voice. Because she tells her own story, Antoinette Cosway does not partake of the conventional mythology: she occupies a central and controlling position, one which eliminates the possibility of her alienation from the established norms of the text. This may be an obvious point, but it is worth stressing, for it allows us to recognize the fundamental impulse of *Wide Sargasso Sea* as a shift of focus rather than an elaborate departure from the personal histories of Rochester and Bertha in *Jane Eyre*. Here Antoinette has a full history that utterly subverts her representation in *Jane Eyre*, or rather, her representation as it is commonly read. Yet in this act of subversion, the later novel does not traduce the earlier. In *Jane Eyre* Rochester relates to Jane the story of his marriage in a speech replete with contempt and disgust:]

I found her nature wholly alien to mine, her tastes obnoxious to me, her cast of mind common, low, narrow, and singularly

incapable of being led to anything higher . . . whatever topic I
started, immediately received from her a turn at once coarse and
trite, perverse and imbecile . . . (p. 333)

By the methods of any critical school concerned with a
close reading of the text it is surely possible if not even
correct, to read this [account] as [Rochester's story and no one
else's, and its veracity, therefore, is open to challenge. Yet
examinations of *Jane Eyre* are rarely, if every, concerned with
examining what may lie behind Rochester's account, which is
unthinkingly accorded the status of an authentic history. Jean
Rhys's reading of *Jane Eyre* will not allow it this status: she
revises but she does not travesty, and her interpretation of the
Rochester in *Jane Eyre* probably attends to such passages as
this as evidence of the character's impetuosity and malice,
rather than evidence of his tragic past. *Wide Sargasso Sea*
strongly suggests that it is unthinking malice and jealousy on
Rochester's part that drives his wife mad, an aggression
incorporated in his tiring of her] Antoinette Cosway is a form
of currency. [Rochester buys her, fittingly, in a land of slave-
trading, and discovers that his newly acquired riches, like
those of the landscape surrounding him, offer him only
temporary pleasures.]
[The images of exploitation that populate Jean Rhys's novel
are also a means of suggesting that its human relations are
governed by the rules and attitudes of commodity exchange.
Thus on making a contract with Antoinette, Rochester is
promptly accosted by Daniel who wishes to exploit the
rumours of her conduct, and the book's final section begins
with Grace Poole's prelude on the financial arrangements of
her employment as keeper. At the centre of the novel's events,
Rochester bitterly complains, 'they bought me, *me* with your
paltry money. You helped them to do it', seeing himself as the
victim, while Christophine sees Antoinette as the loser in the
telling accusation she levels at Rochester:

'She don't come to your beautiful house to beg you to marry with
her. No, it's you come all the long way to her house – it's you beg
her to marry. And she love you and she give you all she have.
Now you say you don't love her and you break her up. What you
do with her money, eh?' Her voice was still quiet but with a hiss

in it when she said 'money'. I thought, of course, that is what all the rigmarole is about. I no longer left dazed, tired, half-hypnotized, but alert and wary, ready to defend myself. (p. 130)

Money governs the situation utterly, and Rochester has readily deferred to its power, as his imaginary letter to his father demonstrates:

Dear Father. Thirty thousand pounds have been paid to me without question or conditions. No provision made for her (that must be seen to). I have a modest competence now. I will never be a disgrace to you or to my dear brother the son you love. No begging letters, no mean requests. None of the furtive shabby manoeuvres of a younger son. I have sold my soul or you have sold it, and after all is it such a bad bargain? (p. 59)

Antoinette's mother is victim too, and her history of great consequence in the establishing of Antoinette's so-called hereditary madness. Stranded after the loss of her estate and the life-style which gave her a meaning,[11] the insane condition of which she is accused foreshadows Antoinette's circumstances with Rochester, for Mason hires keepers (as Rochester hires Grace Poole) and maintains her in the country. But when Antoinette goes to see her mother, she finds not madness but the rejection of the daughter who has come in the place of the crippled son, the dead Pierre:

She looked at the door, then at me, then at the door again. I could not say, 'He is dead,' so I shook my head. 'But I am here, I am here,' I said, and she said 'No,' quietly. Then 'No no no' very loudly and flung me from her. (p. 40)

After this, she goes again, and her account of her second visit has an important place in her narrative, for it forms a part of the true story of her mother's conditions which she gives Rochester in an attempt to disabuse him of the opinions gleaned from the rumours about her. She relates how she looked into the room where her mother was confined, how her mother was offered rum, and how she walked about distracted by memories of her former life, evident in her broken phrases:

Then she seemed to grow tired and sat down in the rocking-chair. I saw the man lift her up out of the chair and kiss her. I saw his mouth fasten on hers and she went all soft and limp in his arms and he laughed. The woman laughed too, but she was angry. (p. 111)

This is one of the few glimpses we get of Antoinette's mother in her confinement, and an essential one therefore in providing a clue as to the nature of her malady, her treatment, and the real source of the rumours which surround her, and eventually, Antoinette. Antoinette's mother is a point at which many of the novel's images of exploitation and prejudice converge. A figure representative of the former white oppression, she finds herself now the subject of the islander's revenge as well as her husband's malice. Once herself subjugated by the oppressive class (although herself a member of it) she is now a scapegoat, oppressed and victimized as a woman. Her estate burnt, her son killed, she is now kept and subjected to sexual exploitation. It is here, then, that the rumours of intemperance and loose living originate, and they are taken up and embroidered by Daniel, who wishes to avenge himself on her community and family. This confined woman, once 'marooned' (her own word) on her crumbling estate and in her marriage to the drunken Cosway, subsequently maintained as a kept woman by Mason, provides the emblematic history of imprisonment and alleged madness in which Antoinette's life will also be traced. After the fire and Pierre's death she will have nothing to do with Mason, and this grief in isolation (in accordance with the romantic pattern) condemns her as mad, and thus she is confined as an object to be taunted and appropriated. Like Antoinette after her, she has initial value as capital and property, but once this ceases (Antoinette signs her rights away in the marriage contract) her desires and griefs have no meaning and power, and her inner life – an essential concern of this novel – is denied by the other characters as devoid of value or claims.

Antoinette knows her condition is to be read in terms of her mother's, and that is why she tells her mother's story to Rochester. But Rochester does not want to listen, even though his resistance is broken by Antoinette's telling complaint: 'You have no right to ask questions about my mother and then refuse to listen to my answer' (p. 107). Yet even though the story of the woman's madness is allowed to run its course, Rochester's refusal to understand is still in evidence:

> After a long time I heard her say as if she were talking to herself, 'I have said all I want to say. I have tried to make you understand. But nothing has changed.' She laughed.
> 'Don't laugh like that, Bertha.'
> 'My name is not Bertha; why do you call me Bertha?' (p. 111)

Because he does not listen, Rochester does not recognize Antoinette's true place and identity within the story, and the refusal to acknowledge her history is registered in his insistence in using the name by which he has chosen to possess her. His response is similar when Christophine tells of Antoinette's mother's alleged madness later in the novel.[12]

Wide Sargasso Sea replaces Bertha Mason's monstrous madness with Antoinette Cosway's history of exploitation, prejudice and abuse, a history which carefully charts her state of mind through her relations with Rochester into the almost indiscernible shift into derangement in the final halucinatory pages when she sets fire to Thornfield Hall in her dream. In Jean Rhys's novel madness is not an essential difference: whereas *Jane Eyre* centralizes its values so firmly around its eponymous heroine as to insist on Bertha fulfilling the role of negative to Jane's positive, *Wide Sargasso Sea* will not invest sanity or normality with the dominating presence that is able to define the antitheses of abnormality or madness. It is true that the reader who begins the novel expecting to discover the drama of 'Bertha Mason's' madness will not be disappointed. There is a certain neurotic quality about her vivid yet fragmented and disordered apprehensions of the world around her. Yet this is not a special quality of Antoinette's narrative. Similar and related qualities are encountered in Rochester's section of the novel, and the reader soon realises that the influences of place, situation and atmosphere upon the perceptions of the mind is one of the text's prime concerns. This in turn, being manifested in a series of responses common to Antoinette and Rochester, will not permit the easy or casual demarcation of difference. Additionally, Rochester's narrative is infused with dream-like qualities and broken sequence partly as a consequence of the modernist idiom, and partly because of the probability that for a good proportion of the time he is drunk or feverish. Again, the text is breaking the deadlocked antithetical relation between sanity and insanity proposed by *Jane Eyre*.

In Charlotte Brontë's novel, Jane sees Bertha Mason, significantly, reflected in the mirror, as she tries on the wedding veil in Jane's room. Looking at that image in the mirror, Jane does not recognise her angry self in the 'savage face' and likens it to the visage of a vampire (p. 311). The image proves difficult to repress, yet with some doubts, Jane agrees that Rochester's explanation of what she has seen as 'half-dream, half-reality' is 'the only possible one'. There is a mirror-scene in *Wide Sargasso Sea* too, which takes place in a scene of 'half-dream, half-reality': Antoinette's vision of setting fire to Thornfield Hall. Leaving the attic, she will not look behind her for fear 'of the ghost of a woman whom they say haunts this place'. Later, she sees the 'ghost' in the mirror hung in the hall:

> I went into the hall again with the tall candle in my hand. It was then that I saw her – the ghost. The woman with streaming hair. She was surrounded by a gilt frame but I knew her. I dropped the candle I was carrying and it caught the end of a tablecloth and I saw flames shoot up. (p. 154)

This is the recognition of self, the reclamation of a former life which inspires Antoinette to her act of revenge. As she dreams of destroying Thornfield, so too she evokes elements of her life at Coulibri: Tia, the patchwork, the parrot (which, like Antoinette, dies leaping from a burning building, its wings clipped in its confinement). Watching the sky, she recognizes 'all [her] life in it' (p. 155) and having recovered her history, she is impelled to complete the cycle of destruction which began with the burning of Coulibri itself.

Literature's most famous madwoman is the sacrifice *Jane*

Eyre makes in its tracing of its heroine's virtues. Her madness does not simply heighten the mystery of Rochester's past or excuse his plan to marry Jane, it is the novel's means of distinguishing desires, of discriminating between what it takes to be licentiousness and virtue. Bertha's desires are articulated in the history which punishes her with madness, whereas Jane is apparently desexualized in her attraction to Rochester, who sees her as a 'sunny-faced girl . . . a beauty the desire of my heart – delicate and aerial' (pp. 287–8). Without the detail of Bertha's madness being prematurely induced by her excess, this would not have been the case, but that detail entangles insanity with depravity. The monstrous beast in the attic is indeed a tragic and terrifying symbol of the lost and alienated mind, but she is also an incarnation of excessive and 'wrongful' desire, so clearly emblematized in her assault on Rochester.

Wide Sargasso Sea retrieves the madwoman from this position, sensing how Charlotte Brontë's text finds itself caught in the ideology which produced the double standard. The new history for Bertha/Antoinette is not just a matter of indulgence or speculation, for it is founded with unerring precision on a highly aware critical reading of *Jane Eyre*. In taking up Rochester's accusation that Bertha was 'intemperate and unchaste' and in weaving its psychological and eventful narratives around the implications of this stigma, *Wide Sargasso Sea* is both novel and criticism. The insane woman now occupies the centre of the text, and in that position she exposes the sleight of hand which accepts the conflation of normality and rectitude with a specifically patriarchal code of 'proper' desire.

Notes

1. Charlotte   Brontë,   *Jane   Eyre*,   edited   by   Q. D.   Leavis (Harmondsworth, 1966), p. 334. All references and quotations are from this edition, and page references follow in parentheses.
2. The most rewarding discussion is to be found in Sandra Gilbert and Susan Gubar, *The Madwoman in the Attic: The Woman Writer and the Nineteenth Century Literary Imagination* (New Haven and London,

1979). See also Helene Moglen, *Charlotte Brontë: The Self-Conceived* (New York, 1976).

3. Melanie Klein's theory of object relations are structured around notions of infantile development that emphasise the inter-dependence of the internal world and external situations. Ambivalent feelings begin soon after birth with the 'good' breast (providing nourishment) and the 'bad' (refusing it). This splitting of good and bad objects becomes the infant's method of avoiding confusion and aiding development. See Melanie Klein, *The Psycho-Analysis of Children*, translated by Alex Strachey (London, 1949), pp. 213–9, and *New Directions in Psychoanalysis*, edited by Melanie Klein, Paula Heimann and Roger Money-Kyrle (London, 1971), pp. 21–2. For further explanation and discussion, see Elizabeth Wright, *Psychoanalytic Criticism: Theory and Practice* (London and New York, 1984), pp. 79–84.

4. Gilbert and Gubar (1979), pp. 360, 359–60

5. See Jacques Lacan, *Écrites: A Selection*, translated by Alan Sheridan (London, 1977), pp. 1–7.

6. Gilbert and Gubar (1979), p. 339.

7. Ibid., p. 369.

8. 'Of late, Jane – only – only of late – I began to see and acknowledge the hand of God in my doom' (p. 471). See pp. 471–3.

9. Gilbert and Gubar (1979), pp. 338–9. See also Susan Siefert, *The Dilemma of the Talented Heroine* (Montreal, 1978).

10. Jean Rhys, *Wide Sargasso Sea* (Harmondsworth, 1968), p. 152. All references and quotations are from this edition, and page numbers follow in parentheses.

11. See Antoinette's comments on pp. 109–10 ('she was part of Coulibri').

12. Christophine is explicit about the sexual exploitation of Antoinette's mother. When Rochester asks about her madness, Christophine replies, 'They drive her to it. When she lose her son she lose herself for a while and they shut her away. They tell her she is mad. Question, question. But no kind word, no friends, and her husban' he go off, he leave her. They won't let me see her. I try, but no. They won't let Antoinette see her. In the end – mad I don't know – she give up, she care for nothing. They man who is in charge of her he take her whenever he want and his woman talk. That man, and others. Then they have her. Ah there is no God' (pp. 129–30). Rochester then 'wearily' promises Christophine that he will 'do all [he] can' for his wife, but while engaged in this interchange he is thinking of Daniel's calumny.

CHAPTER SIX

Freud's Short Stories:

Tales of Excessive Desire

The inclusion of Freud's writings in this study may initially appear as a violation, a dragging in of a writer who is neither Romantic nor literary, and whose concerns are rarely wide enough to embrace madness itself. In contesting such judgements, a number of points might be made: Freud has been regarded as a literary artist before, a 'great artist' no less; the tradition of medicine to which he belongs might be deemed Romantic, growing out of the German tradition of Schelling's *Naturphilosophie*, a tradition in which mesmerism and ultimately Charcot's hypnotism, played a most significant part; madness is perhaps not so distinct from certain neurotic conditions investigated by Freud.[1] Yet these points, singly or together, do not provide a fitting introduction to why Freud has a place in this book, even while they may open up some interesting preliminary issues.

It is with Freud's work on hysteria that I shall be concerned.[2] In their *Preliminary Communication* which treats of the 'hypnoid states' of hysteria (as distinct from hypnotic therapy, an 'artificial hysteria' induced to cure the primary species) Freud and Breuer characterized these states as a form of madness. Hysterics they claim, may be talented and strong-minded 'but in their hypnoid states they are insane, as we all are in dreams.'[3] Further, they explain that while the 'insanity' of dreaming is confined to sleep, the symptoms of hysteria may be read as an intrusion by the 'products' of hypnoid states into waking life.[4] In this reading, the hysteric's symptoms are signs of a kind of madness, a spilling over of the irrationality of dream or trance into consciousness. Like

many medical writers before him, Freud found no real need
to make a rigorous distinction between madness and hysteria
at this stage in his work: indeed, the symptoms of the latter
malady are defined by way of the more general familiarity
with the former condition, or at least, the common public
notion of it.[5] In that they place insanity and hysteria closely
together, Freud and Breuer are not so distinct from the
nineteenth-century writers referred to earlier in this study.
Moreover, Freud's relations with his patients and the
subsequent texts he produced describing those relations may
be seen as replicating the common pattern or structure with
which I have been repeatedly concerned, that of the
patriarchal text's enclosure of feminine derangement. In this
limited but very real sense, mad women have an important
role to play in Freud's writing.

But is this writing Romantic? Since there is no commonly
agreed working concept of Romantic medicine, I feel free to
begin by exploiting George Rosen's definition of Romantic
medicine as 'the reconstruction of medicine in a period of
revolution'.[6] The description would fit Freud's new map of
human psychology, but at the same time, its flexibility is
weakening, serving all people in all causes. Freud's
connections with Romanticism do not merely hang on his
revolutionary methods and assertions, but on the nature of his
challenges to scientific orthodoxy. Broadly speaking, those
challenges depend upon Freud insisting on establishing
human impulse, drive and need at the centre of his
explicatory models. This involves a hypothetical premise
about the nature of mankind, based on observation and
deduction, but conjectural nevertheless, and therefore a form
of opposition to the prevailing scientific spirit which would
not admit such elements into its practice, a practice based on
the Cartesian model of matter and motion, and explained in
terms of chemical-physical forces. Freud's relation to this
orthodoxy and his relation to Romantic medicine through
Fleiss have been discussed and outlined by Iago Galdston in a
readily available article.[7] I shall simply add that Freud, like
Wordsworth, believed he knew the way to discover
something of mankind's essential nature, and began not with
examples of normality, but with those whose behaviour

denoted disturbance and alienation. Further, Freud may be placed in a position of succession to the therapeutic methodology which characterizes the writings on insanity at the turn of the previous century. I have taken that tradition to be Romantic, and it seems logical therefore, to end this book with a discussion of the most distinguished proponent of the therapeutic treatment of derangement.

As for Freud's credentials for admittance to a discussion largely about fiction and poetry, there should be little dispute. Quite apart from well-founded contemporary unease about 'literature's' exclusive status, there is ample precedent for studying Freud's writerly qualities, and Stephen Marcus's article on 'Dora' points the way clearly enough.[8] But for my purposes, it is unnecessary to look further than Freud himself for justification, for in his discussion of the case of Fräulein Elisabeth Von R., he notes, almost by way of apology:

> It still strikes me myself as strange that the case histories I write should read like short stories and that, as one might say, they lack the serious stamp of science. I must console myself with the reflection that the nature of the subject is evidently responsible for this, rather than any preference of my own. The fact is that local diagnosis and electrical reactions lead nowhere in the study of hysteria, whereas a detailed description of mental processes such as we are accustomed to find in the works of imaginative writers enables me, with the use of a few psychological formulas, to obtain at least some kind of insight into the course of that affection.[9]

In this confession there are a number of interesting manoeuvres. Freud's strategy is to suggest a scientific preference, possibly as a means of appeasing those hostile to his methods. He implies that he has written short stories in spite of himself, drawn by what he calls 'the nature of the subject' – the hysteric, the deranged woman – a sufficiently powerful literary genus to drag him out of a preferred form of discourse into another, hence his surprise. Despite the apology, he finds strengths in his new position, for the discourse of literature offers models for the analysis of the mind. Freud rightly sees himself as an imaginative writer, and he subscribes to his new mode in the way of the Romantic humanist: literature is a way of finding truth, its 'detail' and 'imagination' obtains 'insight'.

I

It has often been my concern to suggest ways in which the myth of the deranged woman is a peculiarly volatile *topos*, a device capable of exceeding and even reversing its apparent brief, capable too, of readily exposing the ideological machinery which produced it. In this sense, the relations between text and sub-text have been the subjects of this study. Freud's short stories present the most interesting and difficult examples of these sets of relations, and because of this, it is as well to begin with a description of the way in which the Case Studies of the *Studies on Hysteria* are arranged.

Each story begins with a text of symptoms, a description of a condition, linked to a simple and brief account of the patient's circumstances and immediate history. The fourth study ('Katharina') is an exception, and its distinctive qualities are discussed later in this chapter. In the first paragraph of 'Fräulein Elisabeth Von R.', however, we learn that her father had died, her mother had an operation, her sister was subsequently ill, and that the burden of nursing these sick relatives had fallen to her, and in the fourth paragraph of 'Frau Emmy Von N.' we receive a fairly full account of her life so far:

> Her family came from Central Germany, but had been settled for two generations in the Baltic Provinces of Russia, where it possessed large estates. She was one of fourteen children, of which she herself is the thirteenth. Only four of them survive. She was brought up carefully, but under strict discipline, by an over-energetic and severe mother. When she was twenty-three she married an extremely gifted and able man who had made a high position for himself as an industrialist on a large scale, but was much older than she was. After a short marriage he died of a stroke. To this event, together with the task of bringing up her two daughters, now sixteen and fourteen years old, who were often ailing and suffered from nervous troubles, she attributed her own illness. (p. 105)

This story, or sequence of events, set within the present context of the patient's hysterical condition, has no plot in the Aristotelian sense. Here a false plot is offered: the woman attributes her illness to the wrong set of circumstances. Something else, therefore, has to be forthcoming if we are to understand the sequential relations of the story being offered to the reader. Moving from this primary text, the hysterical symptoms and the skeleton history, Freud seeks to supply a plot of causal interrelation. He will supply the missing elements of the story which will ultimately explain or rationalize the relation of its elements. In the structure here beginning to evolve, the patient is an author whose intended utterances are an unsatisfactory explication or resolution of their relations and meanings. What is needed is a sub-text that the patient as author cannot supply given the constraints of the presently employed form (that of conscious utterance) and Freud as critic or even co-author can supply this through hypnosis or therapy. In this first re-reading of the story, Freud's prompting and questioning combine with the patient's accounts and answers to achieve an abreaction which recovers the missing elements to make up a new plot. Finally a fuller text emerges out of these new explanations and the history as initially rendered. This is Freud's short story: the impersonal account of life so far plus the woman's own narrative delivered under the conditions of hypnosis or interrogation. Freud not only supplies the deranged woman's story, he suggests she is telling it herself.

Yet this is not all. While the text of the short story is now fuller, an elaboration of the documentary history, it is supplemented by yet another text, an analysis which Freud provides and calls the 'Discussion'. This is the second re-reading, and again the mode is of a specifically literary kind. After the narrative is seemingly complete, a new voice emerges intent on framing its events, supplementing absences not perceived in the first re-reading, or perhaps stressing new moments of significance. The discussion is not only an accumulation of more meaning in itself, but also an invitation to the reader to interpret. The technique is redolent of Poe's short stories in particular:

If someone were to assert that the present case history is not so much an analysed case of hysteria as a case solved by guessing, I should have nothing to say against him.

It will be understood that I speak of coincidences and *no more*. What I have said upon this topic must suffice. In my own heart there dwells no faith in praeter-nature.[10]

In both examples the writer is intent on extending the discourse beyond the narrative. There is an anticipation (disingenuous or otherwise) of the reception – 'If someone were to . . .', 'It will be understood . . .' – and a suggestion that the most obvious interpretation is clearly not the right one. This is a critical act, a re-reading in Barthes's sense,[11] that is set upon establishing a new or unique response to a narrative whose events are not so new nor so unique. As events in a story they are commonplace, readily drawn from the history of social life, and while they may be arranged into interesting patterns, it requires an act of re-reading (criticism) to denote the text's difference from that already known. Barbera Johnson, following Barthes, puts it most succinctly:

a single reading is composed of the already-read, . . . what we see in a text the first time is already in us, not in it; in us insofar as we ourselves are a stereotype, an already-read text; and in the text only to the extent that the already-read is that aspect of a text that it must have in common with its reader in order for it to be readable at all. . . . The statement that those who do not reread must read the same story everywhere involves a reversal of the usual properties of the words *same* and *different*. Here it is the consuming of different stories that is equated with the repetition of the same, while it is the rereading of the same that engenders what Barthes calls the 'text's differences'.[12]

By its very act of interposition, criticism presupposes the unsatisfactory condition of the reader primed for the text by what is already known, and ready to receive it therefore, according to the coincidences occurring between his or her knowledge and that seemingly proposed by the text. Criticism expects the first reading to be a parapraxis, and demands a re-reading in the form of analysis.

When applied to texts that do not overtly contain their own

acts of criticism in series or in supplements, this critical model seems straightforward enough. Obviously though, re-readings are infinite, and the factor of infinity applies doubly when confronted with texts which do perform their own critical acts, such as those under consideration here. I am here trying to re-read Freud's 'Case Histories' which already contain two re-readings of their own (in most cases) and self-consciously protective ones at that, concerned to tie down the play of signification, and guide the reader into the psychoanalytical theory that will eventually resolve the questions surrounding the narrative itself. It is as well to begin then, by sorting out the nature of the relation of Freud's short story (history plus narrative) and the succeeding piece of criticism or commentary (discussion).

Why does Freud make this separation? Breuer's narratives are altogether different in this respect. The answer Freud offers is incomplete, but demonstrates something of the nature of his difficulties:

> Case histories of this kind are intended to be judged like psychiatric ones; they have, however, one advantage over the latter, namely an intimate connection between the story of the patient's suffering and the symptoms of his illness – a connection for which we still search in vain in the biographies of other psychoses.
>
> In reporting the case of Fraulein Elisabeth von R. I have endeavoured to weave the explanations which I have been able to give of the case into my description of the course of her recovery. It may perhaps be worthwhile to bring together the important points once more. (p. 231)

The story provides intimacy, removing the case-study from the experimental conditions of the clinic and placing it in the wider arena of social history. This is the first and perhaps most essential point to which I shall return. Secondly, Freud proposes the virtues of reiteration. In this instance this is indeed what follows, but there is much else besides, for the discussion allows him to expand the discourse into theoretical conjecture and generally or scientifically observed 'truths'. Thus, according to conversion theory, 'she repressed her erotic idea from consciousness and transformed the amount of its affect into physical sensations of pain' (p. 235) or, at a simpler level, 'there are good reasons for the fact that sick-nursing plays such a significant part in the prehistory of cases of hysteria' (p. 232). Yet Freud will go much further. Here the discussion also becomes the platform for the delivery of more stories, those of Fräulein Mathilda H., Fräulein Rosalia H., and Frau Cäcilie M.[13] In this the last case-study of the series, the discussion, intent on asserting the text's difference and preventing its assimilation into the already-known, finds itself engaged in asserting its sameness by way of the construction of similar narratives. The construction of the new orthodoxy needs a general base, and demands therefore that the newness or difference of Freud's short stories should establish itself as truthful by an act of multiplication. In protesting that his cases are not singular, Freud resolves textual difference into general truth.

In order for this to be accomplished, the first narrative (the short story) has to stand as an autonomous whole: it must be privileged as a different text before its difference can then be fortified with sameness. For similar reasons, the case-studies selected as stories carry only so much theoretical lumber as they can stand *as stories*. The rest is left to the discussion. Thus each study has a somewhat disingenuous naturalistic guise, appearing as a story from true life, a spontaneously narrated series of events innocently combined in a conventional fictive form. Ultimately though, in part or in parcel, the stories are deprivileged as the observations upon them (I am thinking primarily of the discussions, but also of Breuer's six theoretical essays and Freud's 'The Psychotherapy of Hysteria') extract the relevant details serving as evidence for the construction of a theoretical diagnosis and appropriate treatment. They become supplementary to the science of psychoanalysis, here evolving with fascinating certainty before our eyes. It is as if Freud needs the rhetoric of fiction to allow his case-studies constant reference to the common notions of social life, yet in employing the techniques of the short story, he sets into motion the play of signification that it is the discussion's task to harness and close down.

II

Because of the nature of their enterprise, Freud and Breuer speak for the woman, they mediate the woman's story. It is the manner of the mediation which is so remarkable, for these are very 'writerly' stories, self-consciously intent on inflating the woman's text beyond its mediocre mode and meaning. A quotation from Freud will serve as an illustration.

> Here, then, was the unhappy story of this proud girl with her longing for love. Unreconciled to her fate, embittered by the failure of all her little schemes for re-establishing the family's former glories, with those she loved dead or gone away or estranged, unready to take refuge in the love of some unknown man – she had lived for eighteen months in almost complete seclusion, with nothing to occupy her but the care of her mother and her own pains. (p. 212)

The analyst and artists are here at one: they will produce great things from this simple and commonplace story which Freud suggests would be a 'great disappointment' if offered to a physician treating the patient. Breuer goes further. His judgement of his patient's condition may be bound up with his assessment of her artistic capability:

> I found her in a wretched moral state, inert, unamenable, ill-tempered, even malicious. It became plain from her evening stories that her imaginative and poetic vein was drying up. What she reported was more and more concerned with her hallucinations and, for instance, the things that had annoyed her during the past days. These were clothed in imaginative shape, but were merely formulated in stereotyped images rather than elaborated into poetic productions. (p. 85)

Although Breuer does not produce narrative stories like Freud when writing up his case-studies, there is a similarity in the two men's regard for their patients as muses, yet muses of defective or incompetent kinds. The hysteric, Freud often reminds us, is usually a woman of talent. Not only is she 'passionate . . . capable of strong feelings', but her condition is 'compatible with an unblemished character and a well-governed mode of life' (p. 165). This kind of regard for the patient, which causes Freud to relate of Frau Emmy Von N. that her 'moral seriousness . . . intelligence and energy . . . were no less than a man's' (p. 165), tends also to place his subjects in the mould of the nineteenth-century novel's heroine.[14] They are gifted women of great but often frustrated abilities, yet women still, and prone to what he regards as feminine foibles and weaknesses of mind. In this sense they are permanently in need of the act of completion, and their hysteria is a form of continuous evidence for their dependency, here evinced in the very act of writing the text. These stories of their lives are beyond their own self-knowledge. Their utterances will be transcribed into the coherence of fiction. The muse's story needs re-telling and refining, and the process involves a re-defining of herself to herself by the man, who as messianic analyst is both poet and healer, a truly new Apollo.

In the genesis of Freud's psychoanalysis it is perhaps surprising to find assumptions about hysteria and woman's derangement that partake so fully of the old mythology. As a fictional and medical author, Freud is entirely conventional in the assumptions he makes about the origins of woman's disturbances in her occupations. A powerful mind allowed to wander is considered to be highly dangerous:

> We have nothing new to say on the question of the origin of these dispositional hypnoid states. They often, it would seem, grow out of the day-dreams which are so common even in healthy people and to which needlework and similar occupations render women especially prone. (p. 64)

Reminiscent of the literary satirical tradition and the educational psychiatric writings of the earlier part of the century, the occupational reference is a means of placing the woman in a familiar cultural position. The 'Preliminary Communication' continues to assert that among hysterics 'may be found people of the clearest intellect, strongest will, greatest character and highest critical power' and presents the malady – albeit in a newly sophisticated manner – as a confusion between reality and fantasy. This of course is the common problem of the fictional heroine of the nineteenth century novel, whose development through the text is usually marked by the wisdom growing out of disillusionment, the erosion of youthful ideals by the experience of life (Marianne Dashwood, Lucy Ashton, or the remarkably sane Dorothea Brooke). There is something punitive in the novel's chastening of these heroines, and the course of their action implies that early ambitions were not innocent wants but excessive desires, the excess being denoted through the improperness of trespassing beyond the conventional limits of womanhood as defined by their different situations. In Freud's writings on hysteria, closely related notions are at play. Thus as previously noted, the talented hysteric's qualities may be 'no less than a man's' yet her giftedness may also result in 'an excessive demand for love' and moreover an 'independence of . . . nature which [goes] beyond the feminine ideal' to find expression in 'a considerable amount of obstinacy, pugnacity, and reserve' (p. 231). This characterization occurs in Freud's assessment of Fräulein Elisabeth Von R. which is by no means intended to be unsympathetic. Indeed, Freud protests early in the account that the details of her circumstances were such that 'we cannot refrain from deep human sympathy' (p. 212), and the studies as a whole are concerned to contest theories which saw hysteria as a consequence of degeneration. Yet despite this regard for his patient's qualities, Freud still sees them as prey to excessive desire, perhaps because the activity of writing presents him with ready-made tropes for depicting them in this way. In the case of Fräulein Elisabeth Von R., this is particularly obvious, for her characterization depends heavily on her dissatisfaction with the role she is expected to play as a woman. The relevant passage needs to be quoted in full:

Although the girl's mind found intellectual stimulation from this relationship with her father, he did not fail to observe that her mental constitution was on that account departing from the ideal which people like to see realised in a girl. He jokingly called her 'cheeky' and 'cock-sure', and warned her against being too positive in her judgements and against her habit of regardlessly telling people the truth, and he often said she would find it hard to get a husband. She was in fact greatly discontented with being a girl. She was full of ambitious plans. She wanted to study or to have a musical training, and she was indignant at the idea of having to sacrifice her inclinations and her freedom of judgement by marriage. As it was, she nourished herself on her pride in her father and in the prestige and social position of her family, and she jealously guarded everything that was bound up with these advantages. The unselfishness, however, with which she put her mother and elder sisters first, when an occasion arose, reconciled her parents completely to the harsher side of her character. (pp. 207–8)

This hovers uncertainly between flattery and condemnation: ambition and ability are apparently to be admired and yet they result in jealousy, indignation and finally harshness. The values by which these characteristics are to be judged remain largely unstated. Here, particularly, the difficulty of interpretation is compounded by the relationship between analyst and patient. Inevitably, Freud's role of protagonist and writer exacts demands upon the analysee who ideally complies with the procedures to produce the text. This perfect model does not emerge however, and as a result Freud's writing finds itself slipping into a conventional characterisation:

> During this first period of her treatment she never failed to repeat that she was still feeling ill and that her pains were as bad as ever; and, when she looked at me as she said this with a sly look of satisfaction at my discomfiture, I could not help being reminded of old Herr von R.'s judgement about his favourite daughter – that she was often 'cheeky' and 'ill-behaved'. But I was obliged to admit that she was in the right. (p. 213)

The final addendum is of course a disclaimer, indicating something of Freud's awareness of the immensely difficult and sensitive nature of the analyst's relation with the patient, an awareness to be articulated at a later stage of his career. Here however, the father of this text subsumes the real father's 'text' of his daughter. The act of writing the story, working at this stage in the mode of a diary or an anecdotal personal record readily gathers the trope of the spoilt daughter into its progress, and while it also makes some attempt to repress its influence (in the disclaimer) it has still allowed egress to the impulses of the authoritarian father. Freud identifies himself with Herr Von R. in recalling his judgement and he operates now as surrogate father, frustrated in his over-determined attempts to wrest from the daughter the conduct and most importantly the text he desires. Moments such as these, as I have implied, led Freud into a recognition of transference in the process of analysis: here Freud sees the daughter as transferring to him something of her rebellion against her father, enacted perhaps, in the intimate mode of the father–daughter relationship which Freud has already described. He does not consciously register this. As a consequence, counter-transference takes place as the analyst willingly accepts the role and the judgement which goes with it. But I am less interested in the development of psychoanalysis than in the development of this particular text, which takes up the figure of the spoilt child and then finds itself unable to erase it, even while endorsing the opinion offered by Fräulein Elisabeth as she achieves her small victory. It is perhaps inevitable that Freud's characterizations of his patients should make reference to recalcitrance or obstinacy. He is, after all, concerned to prise from them the stories they know but do not want to hear. Nevertheless, the construction of the 'Case Histories' depends heavily upon the woman being represented at some point as obdurate, so that later she may be transformed. Thus Katharina is 'sulky', Miss Luxy R. is 'laconic' and Frau Emmy Von N. in rebellion is 'ungracious'. These women are not wholly characterized by these descriptions. On the contrary, Freud usually finds considerable space to praise their qualities. But the woman's unwillingness plays an essential part in the stories' development, forming the turning point from which Freud retrieves his patients to normality and amenable temper.

Fräulen Elisabeth Von R.'s story is entirely conventional in its denouement which resolves the events in such a way as to suggest the restitution of the woman to her proper place:

> In the spring of 1894 I heard that she was going to a private ball for which I was able to get an invitation, and I did not allow the

opportunity to escape me of seeing my former patient whirl past in a lively dance. Since then, by her own inclination, she has married someone unknown to me. (p. 230)

Against former inertia, obdurance and hysteric paralysis is set the whirl of the dance, time-honoured signifier (if I may be forgiven the obvious allusion) of matrimony and the cultural harmony of marriage. This story therefore charts the woman's progress from the troubled early life in which independence struggles to find a purchase in the conditions under which she exists, through the taming of analysis to eventual social restoration. 'Fräulein Elisabeth Von R.' is singular in offering a fully-resolved conclusion, and the other stories present endings of a different kind, while charting developments of a similar nature. 'Frau Emmy Von N.' has two endings, one in the text itself and one in the discussion, the first indicating the narrator's increasing distance from the subject of his story, the second (given in a footnote added in 1924) telling of her daughter's intention of take legal proceedings against her. I regard this note as simply a matter of reportage.

The first ending, however, has a very specific function:

Finally, in the summer of 1893, I had a short note from her asking my permission for her to be hypnotized by another doctor, since she was ill again and could not come to Vienna. At first I did not understand why my permission was necessary, till I remembered that in 1890 I had, at her own request, protected her against being hypnotized by anyone else, so that there should be no danger of her being distressed by coming under the control of a doctor who was antipathetic to her, as had happened at ——berg ... I accordingly renounced my exclusive prerogative in writing. (p. 145)

The detail is intriguing. One explanation of its presence might be that it is yet another example of Freud's wish to stress his hypnotic powers,[15] yet while this may be true, there is no doubt that it serves as a suitably stylish complementary ending to his story. For the hypnotic power here renounced is that by which the desired narrative has been elicited, and now that the narrator's triumph is seemingly complete, he feels free to cast aside his privilege. The hypnotic control is consubstantial with authorial omniscience, and the final surrender of 'exclusive prerogative' is not therefore simply that of the analyst, but also that of the author. The second ending supplied in 1924 bears this out, for it makes no further claims upon the subject. Rather than the grandiloquent flourish of the original ending, we have a simple open commentary:

> She was intending to take legal proceedings against her mother, whom she represented as a cruel and ruthless tyrant. It seems that she had broken off relations with both her children and refused to assist them in their financial difficulties. The daughter who wrote to me had obtained a doctor's degree and was married. (pp. 167–8)

Life goes on therefore, but the details of this continuing narrative can be of no real interest to Freud. Those acquainted with the story of Frau Emmy von N. will know that Freud arrested the tale at an impasse that may only be surmounted by the importing of concepts and ideas that the patient herself will not offer – even in hypnosis. Here the discussion begins to play a crucial explicatory role, moving in on the text to fix its meaning in the absence of the desired narrative being produced under hypnosis. In a sense the story's impasse is a disingenuous one, for Freud has set up a mystery to be solved, and he will solve it in the discussion by reference to Frau Emmy's sexual abstinence.

There are reasons for Freud's location of the mystery's key in the discussion. Frau Emmy's story is concerned to focus atention primarily on phobias and their derivation, and in themselves contain only slight elements suggesting traumas of an erotic kind.[16] Moreover, this study is too early for Freud to use the suggestive technique, it being the first instance of his cathartic method. As the patient shows signs of withdrawal, Freud renounces the privilege of control, and this is equally a closing-down of one system of discourse in order to deflect into another. Frau Emmy's telling of her own story has not been a complete success, and Freud admits in the course of this study that 'an incomplete story under hypnosis produces no therapeutic effect'; he develops this by asserting that no improvement in the patient's condition in itself is indicative of the incompleteness of the story she has told. Freud cannot resolve the story and close it down within the terms offered by Frau Emmy's narrative, and in order to insist on the potency of the structuring absence (sexual abstinence) he must surrender the fiction and move to the discussion wherein he can fix the significance of his patient's history:

> In my opinion, however, all these physical factors, though they may account for the *choice* of these phobias, cannot explain their *persistence*. It is necessary, I think, to adduce a *neurotic* factor to account for this persistence – the fact that the patient had been living for years in a state of sexual abstinence. Such circumstances are among the most frequent causes of a tendency to anxiety. (p. 148)

Frau Emmy von N., in not giving utterance to the struggle Freud assumes she has had with her sexual needs, is thus passed on to another doctor, and possibly passed on therefore into another fiction, a text of her history and present needs. Freud has turned from author into critic in order to arrest the meaning of his text, which he now insists is a censored one:

> It has also struck me that among all the intimate information given me by the patient there was a complete absence of the sexual element, which is, after all, more liable than any other to provide occasion for traumas. It is impossible that her excitations in this field can have left no traces whatever; what I was allowed to hear was no doubt an *editio in usum Delphini* of her life story. (pp. 164–5)

The woman without the man is naturally inclined to hysteria in this reading, naturally 'helpless' (among the handicaps Frau Emmy suffers, according to Freud, is the 'natural helplessness of a woman'). While his later work as an analyst developed means of documenting the centrality and power of sexual neuroses, these early studies use the woman's sexual abstinence far more presumptuously. It is part of the written heritage of medical writings with which Freud may have been acquainted, a small part of which has been drawn to the attention of the reader of this book in Chapter 2.[17] It is also part of the literary heritage, where it operates implicitly as a code rather than as an explicit statement. In detecting something akin to this code at work in the story he has produced, Freud is happy to use his credentials as a medical writer and scholar to draw it out into the open. At this point in his writings, these assumptions about the woman alone are less a consequence of Freud's scientific studies as they are a consequence of his cultural inheritance.

The story of Miss Lucy R. offers a much more subdued version of Freud's assumptions or theories of sexual neuroses, yet the interest centres on the patient's unrequited love for her employer. Again the woman's secret desire is that which will explain her disturbance and the events of the narrative. Miss Lucy is presented as a more willing informant, or perhaps more accurately, a more responsive subject to Freud's detective work. This study is structured in the mode of the detective story, Freud exemplifying his deductive skills and building to the climax at which the mystery is solved:

> Now I already knew from the analysis of similar cases that before hysteria can be acquired for the first time one essential condition must be fulfilled: an idea must be *intentionally repressed from consciousness* and excluded from associative modification. In my view this intentional repression is also the basis for the conversion . . . I accordingly inferred from Miss Lucy R.'s having succumbed to hysterical conversion at the moment in question that among the determinants of the trauma there must have been one which she had sought intentionally to leave in obscurity . . . only one conclusion could be reached. I was bold enough to inform my patient of this interpretation. (p. 181)

This is the moment at which Freud accuses Lucy R. of excessive desire, the harbouring of her impossibly ambitious love for the man who employs her as a governess. Not only does she readily confess to this, but she does so in terms confirming the presence of repressed knowledge – 'I wanted to drive it out of my head and not think of it again; and I believe latterly I have succeeded' (p. 181).

The medical interest of 'Miss Lucy R.' is to stress that

hysteria may be acquired, and to depress the significance of pre-existing disposition. To explain this kind of hysteria for which Miss Lucy R. will serve as the model, Freud uses the discussion to stress the significance of the story in terms of the theory he builds of the developed incompatibility 'between the ego and some idea presented to it' (p. 187) and of the subsequent mechanism of conversion. As a result of this purpose, the fictional interest of the story leans towards this incompatibility heavily. Perhaps because of the literary precedents, it is able to do this with ease, able also to coincide its medical or therapeutic purpose with a time-honoured fictional morality in the structure of the *dénouement* which replaced Lucy on her expected social level.[18] When Freud inquires of her prospects in the house, she replies: 'I am quite clear on that subject, I know I have none, and I shan't make myself unhappy over it'; and when asked if she is still in love, she gives an affirmative response, adding that this is something she can control and keep to herself (p. 186). In this the final stage of the story, Miss Lucy is described as transfigured into a state of happiness.

There are good fictional precedents for this, and *Jane Eyre* is perhaps the most obvious, offering an identical social model in the relationship between an independent-minded governess and a violently disposed and dominant employer. Where *Jane Eyre* upsets the social expectation that governesses ought to know better, Freud's story does not, but there is a coincidence between Lucy's resolve to see her hopes as entirely false and the episode in *Jane Eyre* when Jane sketches the portraits of herself and Blanche Ingram as a reminder of her error in seeing Rochester as her lover – 'I had rejected the real, and rapidly devoured the ideal' (p. 190). By painting the portraits she engages in her own therapy which she regards as 'wholesome discipline' leading her back to normality and the ability to meet 'subsequent occurrences with a decent calm' (p. 191). Lucy similarly, after responding to the therapy which not only locates and discloses her secret desire but also the traumas which signify its certain frustration, wakes after the final session with the weight removed from her mind, and continues, we are given to understand, in good spirits. She has therefore escaped what

Freud understands as a developing hysterical condition, a
state of being which Jane Eyre saw in rather more dramatic
terms as the pathway to madness:

> It does good to no woman to be flattered by her superior, who
> cannot possibly intend to marry her; and it is madness in all
> women to let a secret love kindle within them, which, if
> unreturned and unknown, must devour the life that feeds it; and,
> if discovered and responded to, must lead *ignus fatuus*-like, into
> miry wilds whence there is no extrication. (p. 190)]   Isa Craig.

Given the different circumstances and ostensible purposes
of the two texts I am comparing here, it is perhaps remarkable
to discover how readily the common plot of each narrative
provokes a moral polemic on woman's weakness. Freud's
commentary is more restrained but similar in kind, and it
drags his discussion unmistakably into the area of woman's
social responsibility:

> Thus the mechanism which produces hysteria represents on the
> one hand an act of moral cowardice and on the other a defensive
> measure which is at the disposal of the ego. Often enough we
> have to admit that fending off increasing excitations by the
> generation of hysteria is, in the circumstances, the most
> expedient thing to do; more frequently of course, we shall
> conclude that a greater amount of moral courage would have
> been of advantage to the person concerned. (p. 188)

Here Freud is using his discussion in a new way, suddenly
inclining his story at an angle that allows it to be intersected
by a moral reading. Given this comment, we know he would
have admired Jane Eyre's 'moral courage' in painting her two
pictures. In both narratives, it is the woman's secret life, her
'private theatre' (Breuer's phrase) of desire which is seen as a
prospective course to madness. In both texts, too, this private
theatre is regarded as natural in women, the project of a
capacity for self-delusion. *Jane Eyre*, however, uses its plot to
unsettle and undermine the foundation of this assumption: in
the course of the novel self-delusion detaches itself from
Jane's desire for Rochester and settles instead around her
earlier commitments to good service. The story of Miss Lucy

R. of course cannot allow such a plot to evolve, and in itself this cannot be helped. Yet the discussion proves itself to be at pains to close down any emerging sympathies in the reader that may attach themselves to a more romantic reading of Miss Lucy R.'s story. It is in this way that 'Miss Lucy R.', in conceding to a medical diagnosis that is also a common fictive device (the woman's hopes in love) discloses the common source of both to be ideological, a pervasive assumption which readily attaches itself to the apparent regard for the imaginative and talented woman. When Breuer introduces the habits and character of Fräulein Anna O., he illustrates how this assumption works: the secret life or private theatre is imperceptible from the outside, and while the woman behaves normally, she is in fact steadily moving into her illness, led by her fantasies:

> She embellished her life in a manner which probably influenced her decisively in the direction of her illness, by indulging in systematic day-dreaming, which she described as her 'private theatre'. While everyone thought she was attending, she was living through fairy tales in her imagination; but she was always on the spot when she was spoken to, so that no one was aware of it. She pursued this activity almost continuously while she was engaged on her household duties, which she discharged unexceptionably. I shall presently have to describe the way in which this habitual day-dreaming while she was well passed over into her illness without a break. (p. 74)

The story is familiar enough. Anna O.'s life is 'monotonous' and she turns to her fantasies to escape this tedium and the dominance of her puritanical household. This idea of the bored or oppressed dreaming woman is such a common one that it partakes of the mythical power which allows it to be regarded as a natural state, a state continuous too, with her hysteria. As Breuer indicates in the final sentence of this extract, there is no break between her day-dreaming when well and her illness.

Freud's (and to a lesser extent Breuer's) early writings on hysteria concentrate therefore around a series of tropes readily associated with the deranged or disturbed woman.[19] These highly imaginative, idealistic and altruistic women have stepped out of the nineteenth-century novel into the *Studies on Hysteria* where again they find themselves endangered – yet far more explicitly – by their fantasies, ambitions and desires. Moreover, their illness is traced back to sexual frustration and trauma, and their abstinence signifies the debilitating effects of the loss of the man. In the 'Psychotherapy of Hysteria', the essay which issues out of these case-studies, Freud uses their evidence to oppose the theory of hysteria maintained by the school of Charcot which 'regarded the linking of hysteria with the topic of sexuality as a sort of insult' (p. 342). While conceding that other factors are of pertinence in the aetiology of hysterical affliction, Freud is self-consciously traditionalist in his insistence that the disturbed or frustrated sexual life is the central factor:

> As regards hysteria, however, it follows that disorder can scarcely be segregated from the nexus of the sexual neuroses for the purposes of study, that as a rule, it represents only a single side, only one aspect, of a complicated case of neurosis, and that it is only in marginal cases that it can be found and treated in isolation. We may perhaps say in a number of instances: *a potiori fit denominatio* (i.e. it has been given its name from its most important feature). (p. 342)

Breuer too, in his essay on innate disposition, makes similar claims:

> It is self-evident and it is also sufficiently proved by our observations that the non-sexual affects of fright, anxiety and anger lead to the development of hysterical phenomena. But it is perhaps worth while insisting again and again that the sexual factor is by far the most important and the most productive of pathological results. The unsophisticated observations of our predecessors, the residue of which is preserved in the term 'hysteria' (derived from the Greek word for 'uterus') came nearer the truth than the more recent view which puts sexuality almost last, in order to save the patients from moral reproaches. (p. 328)

In the retrospective viewpoint provided by the history of psychoanalysis, these judgements (whatever doubts there may be about their groundings) will be taken as instinctively correct opinions to be fortified later by more detailed accounts of infantile sexuality and neuroses, and new methods of analysis leading to the discovery of the symbolic language of the unconscious and the interpretative strategies capable of unlocking it. Such a retrospective view will not undervalue the significance of Freud's early studies, nor his mistakes here, for they are the foundations for the development of his greatest discoveries. The centrality of the woman's sexual neurosis, therefore, is the embryonic form of the new account to be given of our unconscious lives. It is not my purpose to challenge the viability of this view, but to offer another which sees the *Studies on Hysteria* not as the beginning of something, nor even as a wrong-headed but massively significant false start (as would some historians of Freud) but as the continuation of the Romantic myth of woman's madness, metamorphosed, but recognizable nevertheless, depending still on tropes and assumptions related to those found in earlier writings. Had Freud not written in his fictional mode here, this would not have been viable. As it is, he needs the naturalistic guise of the short story to provide a new kind of authenticity for a new kind of study.

Nowhere is this more evident than in 'Katharina', remarkable for its literary qualities, but for other reasons too. This is the only study set outside the clinical conditions of the formally arranged talking cure, and it tells the story of a younger and probably poorer woman than those encountered in the other stories. Katharina is about eighteen and works as a waitress, although she is a daughter of the hotel's landlady. It is written in almost uninterrupted dialogue, and tells the tale of a spontaneous encounter. As a result, there is a novel relationship established between Freud and the 'patient', and his delight in the success of his analysis is clearly manifested. Not only is the abreaction relatively easy to effect, but the fact that it constitutes a cure is evident in the transformation which takes place before Freud's eyes – 'She was like someone transformed. The sulky unhappy face had grown lively, her eyes were bright, she was lightened and exalted' (p. 197). Deciding at one point to push the analysis no further, Freud explains his hesitation as a 'debt of gratitude' paid because 'she made it so much easier for me to talk to her than to the prudish ladies of my city practice, who regard whatever is natural as shameful' (p. 198). Yet perhaps the most distinctive feature of this story occurs in the footnote added in 1924, here quoted in full:

> I venture after the lapse of so many years to lift the veil of discretion and reveal the fact that Katharina was not the niece but the daughter of the landlady. The girl fell ill, therefore, as a result of sexual attempts on the part of her own father. Distortions like the one I introduced in the present instance should be altogether avoided in reporting a case history. From the point of view of understanding the case, a distortion of this kind is not, of course, a matter of such indifference as would be shifting the scene from one mountain to another. (p. 201)

What we have therefore in 'Katharina' is the unaltered text, the authentic document of Freud as a young artist who, impressed with the delicacy of his material, perhaps even anxious about it himself, freely employs fictional licence to play down the most volatile element in its source.

Set in the dramatic scenery of the Alps, 'Katharina' records the chance meeting of Freud and what must surely be the most ideal and amenable subject for his early analysis of hysteria. Katharina is not a patient in the usual sense, for she approaches Freud when he is out walking in the mountains. As a result this story is even less like a clinical case-study than the others. The original included the detail of rendering Katharina's utterances in her dialect, and the naturalistic fictional mode is most readily demonstrated by its opening:

> In the summer vacation of the year 189 – I made an excursion into the Hohe Tauern so that for a while I might forget medicine and more particularly the neuroses. I had almost succeeded in this when one day I turned aside from the main road to climb a mountain which lay somewhat apart and which was renowned for its views and for its well-run refuge-hut. I reached the top after a strenuous climb, and, feeling refreshed and rested, was sitting deep in contemplation of the charm of the distant prospect. I was so lost in thought that at first I did not connect it with myself when these words reached my ears: 'Are you a doctor, sir?' But the question was addressed to me, and by the rather sulky-looking girl of perhaps eighteen who had served my

meal and had been spoken to by the landlady as 'Katharina'. To judge by her dress and bearing, she could not be a servant, but must no doubt be a daughter or relative of the landlady's. (p. 190)

The chance encounter, a common opening in fiction and poetry, is here of a peculiarly Romantic, even Wordsworthian kind. The solitary writer, seeking to forget the preoccupations of his knowledge, detaches himself from the life of the city to find solace in the contemplation of scenery and prospect. But once there, he finds himself accosted by a figure whose history he will be forced to discover, a history that will draw him back into the responsibilities of social life. In this traditional way, therefore, the opening of 'Katharina' is intent on suggesting that Freud's diagnosis of the conditions of hysteria is inescapable: like another Romantic hero, Dr Frankenstein, he goes to the Alps to forget, only to be discovered by the creature of his own making, come to reveal its life-story.

Freud's narrative is particularly direct, and only interrupted occasionally by clinical commentary, and the effect is of a reported conversation between a perspicacious man and a remarkable garrulous and relatively uninhibited young woman. This is an accelerated analysis in which the pursuit of the mystery is far from ceremonious. In a rare interpolated passage near the beginning Freud indicates clearly the nature of his suspicions, and he promptly acts upon them:

> I should have to try a lucky guess. I had found often enough that in girls anxiety was a consequence of the horror by which a virginal mind is overcome when it is faced with the world of sexuality.
> So I said: 'If you don't known, I'll tell you how I think you got your attacks. At that time, two years ago, you must have seen or heard something that very much embarrassed you, and that you'd much rather not have seen.' 'Heavens, yes!' she replied, 'that was when I caught my uncle with the girl, with Franziska, my cousin.' (pp. 192–3)

It is a scene of the master-detective at work, the 'lucky guess' being a disingenuous reference to what may be taken as instinctive genius combining with experience. As the history unfolds, however, the incident proves to be only partially responsible for the hysterical symptoms. It is an inadequate explanation for the disgust Katharina feels in her attacks, which is translated into physical sickness, and further, it fails to solve the mystery of the 'awful face' that she hallucinates in these attacks. A new and broader history is needed, and Freud expects its arrival with assured anticipation – 'I told her to go on and tell me whatever occurred to her, in the confident expectation that she would think of precisely what I needed to explain the case' (p. 195). Sure enough, Katharina falls back almost at random to two sets of older stories, the first of an early sexual assault made on her by her 'uncle' as she lay in bed, the second telling of her witnessing evidence suggesting his sexual relations with Franziska. Freud comments that these were remembrances that were not understood until she actually experienced what he would later refer to as the primal scene, and he draws the case to its apparent conclusion by suggesting that with this understanding came the urge to repel the earlier recollections.

The mystery, however, may yet be extended, and Freud's curiosity demands further details, even though the 'confession' is complete. It is an odd moment, brought about perhaps partly by the reliance on dialogue which will not allow conjecture to go unspoken, and partly by the need to reinforce the authenticity of the study by having such conjecture confirmed by Katharina herself. It turns out that there are two further conclusions to come. The second is less dramatic than the first, concerning the source of the mnemonic symbol of the angry face of Katharina's 'uncle's' enraged accusation of her betrayal and his subsequent divorce. The first is rather more significant:

> So when she had finished her confession I said to her: 'I know now what it was you thought when you looked into the room. You thought: "Now he's doing with her what he wanted to do with me that night and those other times." That was what you were disgusted at, because you remembered the feeling when you woke up in the night and felt his body.'
> 'It may well be,' she replied, 'that that was what I was

disgusted at and that that was what I thought.'

'Tell me just one thing more. You're a grown-up girl now and know all sorts of things . . .'

'Yes, now I am.'

'Tell me just one thing. What part of his body was it that you felt that night?'

But she gave me no more definite answer. She smiled in an embarrassed way, as though she had been found out, like someone who is obliged to admit that a fundamental position has been reached when there is not much more to be said. I could imagine what the tactile sensation was which she had later learnt to interpret. Her facial expression seemed to me to be saying that she supposed that I was right in my conjecture. But I could not penetrate further . . . (p. 198)

This passage needs quoting in full because of its extraordinary interchanges. This is Freud at his most tendentious. For a successful abreaction, he needs to impose his interpretation of the connection between Katharina's anxiety and Franziska in the first instance, but what follows may be regarded as superfluous to the treatment, or even a prurient detail.[20] Coming to the conclusion of this story we suddenly find ourselves involved in a narrative relentlessly pursuing the question of whether or not this young virgin felt the contact of her 'uncle's' penis. In order to elicit this detail, the interlocutor turns to his own seductive, coaxing techniques ('You're a grown-up girl now') and the worldly-wise interpretation of knowing looks. This is the real climax to the story, not the solutions offered in the previous paragraphs. The penis is revealed as the key to the mystery, the centre of the story, except of course it remains unspoken, coyly suggested. As a result, the reader may only possess the answer to the mystery by colluding in the language of knowing looks and smiles by which the author asserts his understanding of his subject.

In a series of studies concerned to explain neuroses in terms of the absence of the man (through frustrated desire for the ideal object, sexual abstinence, or as here in 'Katharina' through what is termed 'virginal anxiety') it is perhaps inevitable that an over-literal interpretation of the term phallocentrism might emerge at some point.[21] I shall resist this as a conclusion, not simply because it is a banal point to make alongside the elaborate and sophisticated studies of Freud recently published, but also for other reasons. 'Katharina' I take as the pinnacle of Freud's early studies in hysteria not because of its revelations about the part of the body that Katharina felt, but because it is the study which more than any other comes closest to the short story.

In seeing these pieces as stories, I am not trying to suggest that they are in some way untrue, bogus or deceptive. Against an opposite claim that they are the authentic documents of real experience, however, I would attest the rhetorical nature of Freud's writing. His deliberate move away from the formality of the clinical or medical paper is a move into a new kind of authorship, in which the narrator's intimate knowledge of his subject and her history becomes the main focus of attention. The telling of his story is set upon achieving a common rather than a specialist understanding through conventional fictional figures, characterizations and the organization of the plot into a journey of discovery. In 'Katharina' the aetiology of hysteria is not merely noted or explained but dramatized in such a way as to eventually push the reader into the position of a voyeur as the story recreates her early experience and supplements it with her mature response.

Freud's studies are modelled not on specific literary sources, but on a generic understanding of fictional narrative in which the development of the heroines' lives is charted as a struggle towards self-understanding by way of a realization of the significance which lies within the individual history and a general acceptance of the constraining material and social conditions. It is perhaps this as much as anything else which explains their common pattern: their restraining of ambitions and desires, their implicit or explicit movement towards marriage as cure and completion. In her study of hysteria, Ilza Veith draws our attention to Freud's later awareness that his tracing hysteria's genesis in sexuality was in fact a rediscovery of a much earlier theory.[22] This raises the issue of the genealogy of the *Studies on Hysteria*, and while it is most important to stress that Freud's linking of hysteria to sexuality is of a markedly different kind to early theories making the connection when realized in the context of the development of psychoanalysis, it is nevertheless odd that he did not register his awareness of the coincidence earlier. There may be no direct continuity then, between this work and the studies of the eighteenth and nineteenth centuries (or earlier) which explained hysteria in terms of sexual abstinence. But the writing up of the studies as stories may place them within a tradition which drew its raw materials from the same cultural base, the tradition of the madwoman in Romantic writing, the figure whose history has to be discovered and understood within the context of the narrator's wider understanding.

Notes

1. See Stephen Marcus, 'Freud and Dora: Story, History, Case History', in *Literature and Psychoanalysis*, edited by Edith Kurzweil and William Phillips (New York, 1983), p. 154; Iago Gladston, 'Freud in Romantic Medicine', in *Freud: Modern Judgements*, edited by Frank Cioffi (London, 1973), pp. 103–23.
2. I have chosen not to discuss 'Dora' ('Fragment of an Analysis of a Case of Hysteria') as it is a work which has recently received a considerable amount of critical attention, and is structurally distinct from the earlier studies of 1893–5.
3. Josef Breuer and Sigmund Freud, *Studies on Hysteria*, translated by James and Alix Strachey, edited by James and Alix Strachey, assisted by Angela Richards, *The Pelican Freud Library* (Harmondsworth, 1974), Vol. 3, 64. All references and quotations are from this edition, and page numbers follow in parentheses.
4. In this theory women are particularly vulnerable: 'We have nothing new to say on the question of the origin of these dispositional hypnoid states. They often, it would seem, grow out of the day-dreams which are so common even in healthy people and to which needlework and similar occupations render women especially prone' (p. 64).
5. See also Breuer's comments on p. 331, where he disputes Moebius's disqualification of 'hysterical insanity' to assert that certain hysterical states constitute insanity of a kind.
6. George M. Rosen, 'Romantic Medicine: A Problem in Historical Periodization', *Bulletin of the History of Medicine*, 25 (1951), 149–58, pp. 57–8.
7. Galdston (op.cit.). See particularly 110–12.
8. Freud's own preface to 'Dora' anxiously anticipates a fictional reading, and Hélène Cixous produced a fictional reading intent on 'decentring'

the text in *La jeune née* (1975). See Jane Gallop, *Feminism and Psychoanalysis: The Daughter's Seduction* (London, 1982), pp. 132–8.

9. See p. 231. The literary qualities of Freud's writings and theory were also perceived by the early reviewers of this work, one describing the theory as 'nothing but the kind of psychology used by poets'. See Ernest Jones, *Sigmund Freud, Life and Work*, 2 vols (London, 1956), I, 278–9.

10. Edgar Allen Poe, 'The Mystery of Marie Roget', in *Tales of Mystery and Imagination* (London, 1908), p. 453.

11. Roland Barthes, *S/Z*, translated by Richard Miller (New York, 1974), pp. 15–16.

12. Barbera Johnson, *The Critical Difference* (Baltimore and London, 1980), p. 3.

13. See p. 234 (note); p. 241 (note); pp. 248–55.

14. Here (p. 165) Freud also remarks that the connection between hysteria and giftedness is 'made plain beyond a doubt in the biographies of women eminent in history and literature'.

15. For other examples, see pp. 106, 162.

16. An erotic trauma is narrated nevertheless on p. 138.

17. See note 22.

18. The precedents here are not merely literary, but would also include mythical structures such as those operating in 'Cinderella'.

19. There is, of course, Freud's celebrated case of male hysteria which he presented on 15 October 1886 to the Viennese Society of Physicians. The unfavourable reception may well have derived partly from the lack of an appropriate narrative convention for relating male hysteria. For a recent challenging of the common readings of this incident, see Frank J. Sulloway, *Freud, Biologist of the Mind* (London, 1979), pp. 36–41.

20. See the commentary in Gallop (1982), particularly pp. 38–40.

21. This question is an old one (see Gallop (1982), pp. 16–18) but is also a matter of contention among feminist writers. See Juliet Mitchell's reclaiming of Freud in *Psychoanalysis and Feminism* (Harmondsworth, 1975), particularly pp. 395–8. Gallop's book is a more sustained consideration of phallocentrism in psychoanalysis.

22. Ilza Veith, *Hysteria: The History of a Disease* (Chicago and London, 1970), pp. 264–5.

APPENDIX

Case-Studies

Many nineteenth-century medical writers included details of case histories in their accounts of insanity. In some instances, these were inserted as a separate section of the book, but more often they were to be found as digressions within the chapters themselves, enlisted in the service of proving certain theories, treatments or diagnoses of insanity, or simply contributing authentic details to the descriptions of species of madness or derangement. What is offered here is a selection of these miniature histories, which I see as being stories of a kind, minimal fictions, not in the sense of their being false, but in the sense that they are constructed as narratives. These texts are not commonly available, but may be considered as essential documents in the history of writing women's madness. They are also presented here to supplement the material of Chapter 2.

To a certain extent, the selection is arbitrary, but I have included examples of special relevance to this book (for instance, those dealing with erotomania or disappointed love) and examples that are particularly open to acts of reading and interpretation.

Sir W. C. Ellis M.D., *A Treatise on the Nature, Symptoms, Causes and Treatment of Insanity* (London, 1838)

Ellis argues in this work that insanity derives from the diseased actions in the brain, provoked by a number of causes,

some physical (old age, blows to the head) but most 'moral',
these being defects in reasoning caused by emotional shocks
or behavioural irregularities. Ellis is referred to in Chapter 2.

These five case-studies are taken from Ellis's consideration
of primary moral causes, among which he includes grief and
disappointment in love.

1. pp. 71–4

R. W., a female about forty-five years of age, has been insane
for some time. She lost two or three children very suddenly,
either from fever or small-pox. She was a most affectionate
mother, and became inconsolable for her loss. At the time of
her admission, all the violence of her grief had abated. She
seemed to have forgotten the particular circumstances of their
death, and appeared only conscious of their absence, without
being able to account for it. She used constantly to walk about
the gallery and bedrooms, looking behind every door and into
every corner, expecting to find them; and, if she could wander
into the garden, or about the premises in any direction, her
only business was to seek for her children, and then return,
lamenting her disappointment. By degrees, she was induced
to employ herself. She recovered her health, and ultimately
got quite well, and was discharged about eighteen months
after her admission.

S. T. had been insane two years when admitted. She was
sitting with her husband at breakfast, and remarked to him,
that she thought he appeared unwell; but he said 'No, he was
much as usual.' In a short time she left him, and went
upstairs. She had scarcely gone out of the room, when she
heard a sudden noise, as if something had fallen down; she
immediately ran downstairs, and found that her husband had
fallen out of his chair on the ground and was unable to rise. He
spoke to her, and she ran to the next door, to send some one
for medical assistance; but when she returned, he was a
corpse. In consequence of this sudden bereavement, she was
left with four children entirely destitute. A subscription was
raised on her behalf: but the effect of this sudden shock on the
nervous system produced a depression of spirits so
overwhelming, that she was incapable of attending to
anything: she could obtain no sleep, and was accustomed to

walk the room, in an agony of grief, all the night long. Notwithstanding every kindness that could be shown to her, she became worse, and was ultimately removed to a public hospital, from which she was discharged as incurable. She at length died from pure exhaustion.

H. G., aged thirty-six had only been insane three weeks when admitted. She was in a most distressing state of misery, arising from poverty and remorse. It appears that, some time ago, she was reduced to the most abject beggary, and unable to obtain food for herself and her little boy, who was about four or five years old. Under this pressure, she was induced to sell her child to a chimney-sweeper for a guinea. She had scarcely done the deed before she repented of it; and she set out to find the man, return the money, and reclaim her child. She soon became much excited, she wandered about all night in every direction, but could not hear any tidings of him. In addition to the painful feelings thus naturally produced, she had the mortification either of losing, or of being robbed of the very guinea for which she had sold him: this she considered a just punishment for the crime of which she had been guilty. She continued wandering about from place to place, going to all the chimney-sweepers she could hear of, and making every inquiry, but all in vain. Her child was never found again. The health of the body and powers of the mind, as might be supposed, at length sunk under the united effects of want and anxiety. She was picked up as a lunatic vagrant, and sent to the Asylum at Wakefield, where I left her unimproved, two years after her admission. In this instance, remorse was probably, as much the cause of the insanity, as grief.

2. p. 80

M. T., aged thirty, has been insane for four months. Cause of the attack, disappointment in love. She formed an engagement with a young man, about six years ago; and he left her, after promising marriage. She says, that she has never been comfortable in her mind since, though she has worked regularly until within a few weeks. But she has shown evident symptoms of derangement: she neglected her business, and returned to her friends, saying, her state of mind would not permit her to work. About a week before her admission, she passed a whole night in the street, and she has since meditated self-destruction. Was discharged, cured, in eleven months.

3. pp. 81–2

M. D., thirty years of age, had been insane only a few weeks. She had been brought up as a dressmaker, but unhappily had been seduced by an officer, to whom she was very much attached; after living with him for some time, he deserted her for another. Grief, mortified pride, and jealousy, all combined, produced a state of excitement which ultimately ended in insanity. She had sleepless nights, the natural secretions were disordered, and violent mania was the consequence. It happened unfortunately that my wife had so strong a resemblance to her rival, that nothing could persuade her but that she was the identical person. In consequence of this similarity, whenever she went into her presence her rage knew no bounds. This irritation was avoided as much as possible by the patient being usually shut up in her own room before the former passed through the wards; but on one or two occasions, unfortunately, this precaution had been neglected, and the patient flew upon her with the savageness of a tiger, and literally pulled nearly all the clothes from her person before the nurses could rescue her from her grasp. On a subsequent occasion she accidentally found herself alone with her in an upper gallery used only as a dormitory; she disappeared on a sudden, when my wife instantly ran to the door, and had just time to get through it before she came up. When out of sight she had gone into one of the rooms to get a large leaden pot, with which she said she had intended to murder her. She was not violent against anyone else, and would sometimes even beg of her, as she had got her lover from her, that she would be kind to him. She died of consumption in about two years.

M. Allen, M.D., *Essay on the Classification of the Insane* (London, 1833)

Another doctor practising in asylums, Allen followed the methods of Pinel and Tuke in avoiding restraint and recommending institutions 'not so much for the confinement, as for the cure of the insane' (p. 105). As part of his reforming project in the *Essay*, he included an Appendix of descriptions of what he called the 'old insane', by which he means those patients treated by old methods of restraint, and subsequently not accorded the respect and propriety which he saw as essential means of making the patient feel like a visitor.

The two case-studies given here are taken from Allen's Appendix.

1. pp.¹59–61 (No. 14)

No statement of her case and I have failed in obtaining any very satisfactory information about her.

It is said, that she gradually became insane, after the death of her only boy, named 'Charles' (who was the natural son of Sir ——:) this is probably true, as she now imagines that Charles is constantly with her – sleeps with her – that she feeds him at her meals – carries him about in a corner of her apron – nurses him – and talks to him with delight and maternal fondness. She often fancies, too, that she has been confined and has got more children.

Her appearance and manners are exceedingly polite, pleasing, and affectionate; she is attentive to others, in all those little nameless etiquettes of life, which, when regulated by truth, constitute the innocent fascination of a kind-hearted and well-bred character; and it is so with her: everyone dotes upon her as upon a favourite child. She never fails to tell me, if I have been out during dinner-time, when she next meets me, 'you have not got your dinner, go and get it immediately;' and yet left to herself, she is wholly taken up with scolding some imaginary beings who annoy her, get into her throat, hand, back, &C., run her through with swords, and do a thousand other strange and cruel things to her. Every evening she has a long scolding, with a tone three-fourths of anger and one fourth affection, with some men who plague her in her bed and in her bedroom, and continue to do so till her attendant comes, sometimes at her call, to drive them away. Is this the lingering last impression made on her mind by her seducer? In the midst of her scolding she will often swear in a strange undertone of voice; and when accused, she says it is some other person, frequently Jack Swales. Her conversation is so exceedingly extravagant and varied that it is impossible, except by the most lengthened description, to convey to others any adequate conception of it. Names of dukes, kings, queens, pipes of wine, sums of money, estates, &C., are as common to her as household words; yet strange as all this is, it seems to have some connexion with her past life, having formerly held a situation in a family of consequence. Her former situation and disposition are hinted at by these reminiscences, which are delightful traits of what she has been.

2. pp. 188–90 (No. 24)

Admitted 1802. – Aged twenty five.

Nothing on record. She was brought up tenderly and respectably: her health was rendered delicate by close confinement at her needlework, and her fondness for reading and writing. She was from home when her mind received a severe shock by the unexpected intelligence of her father having put an end to his own existence. Soon after this a grievous disappointment completed the overthrow of her mind. Before her father's death, it was generally supposed he was wealthy: she was then engaged to one who had secured her affections; after her lover knew of her father's death, and the involved state of his affairs, he still continued to profess his attachment, and held out the prospect of speedily fulfilling his promise of marriage; – she believed him, until she happened accidentally in company to cast her eye on the announcement of his marriage to another, when she shuddered and shrieked, and exclaimed 'Wretch!' and from that moment she was insane, and has been so ever since. Her lucid intervals are considerable; yet she always retains so painful a recollection of this fact, that though fond of talking of other occurrence of her former life, she studiously evades all conversation, or any question that at all alludes to this; so much so, that from this fact, as well as some others, I think it highly probable that even her present less violent, and less frequent paroxysms, are partly brought on by associations which awaken the same agony of mind and feelings of indignation as she then suffered. When highly excited, she will, like one who has received some extreme provocation, (her face red and swoln with rage) burst forth into the most violent passion, using the most scurrilous language; sometimes it is maniacal fury; at other times, only like one excessively angry, venting feelings by a hearty scolding; at others, she is only perverse and sulky, and frequently merely odd and flighty. All these symptoms for the most part occur, more or less, at certain periods (see Observation V, and Essay on Atmospheric Influence)* but now they are something less violent at all times, and sometimes, for many months in succession, so slight that strangers could not perceive them, when she continues conversable and pleasant. She is very agreeable and useful in the house, which she considers her home. Perhaps this improvement may be attributed partly to the application of the medical swing – partly to the greater mildness of her present attendant: she is made happy by a little attention, and often visits her friends in York. Her natural talents are good, and improved by reading; her disposition is friendly and benevolent, but hasty, credulous, and incautious.

* Observation V (pp. 127–51) argues for the influence of the seasons and atmospheric change on states of mind, and on insane syndromes or 'periodicity', but Allen is also anxious to stress moral and educational causes in the onset of insanity. Thus as part of this same observation he notes, 'we call it insanity when external restraints are broken down and disregarded; we cannot decide how long absurd and delusive feelings and notions have monopolized all the operations of the little world within. I shall have occasion hereafter to adduce the history of many cases which will serve to illustrate the truth of these views. I may briefly mention, that they occur most frequently in those families where such a constant April atmosphere exists: and, as a further argument it may be stated, that a greater proportion of victims to these causes occur among the women that among the men; and in the male sex we find they are those of a more feminine character, or those whose feelings naturally predominate over their understandings' (p. 146).

Sir Alexander Morison M.D., *The Physiognomy of Mental Diseases,* 2nd edition (London, 1843)*

Morison's *Outlines of Lectures* are referred to in Chapter 2, where an account of some of his ideas about woman's insanity may be found. This odd physiognomical study is perhaps best introduced in Morison's own words, taken from his prefatory remarks: 'The delineations given in this work intended to exhibit the effect of delusions and of strong propensities upon the physiognomy, as well as that of deficiency of intellect and of emotion in depriving the countenance of expression have been selected with care, and the likenesses have been taken under my direction by Messrs F. Rochard, A. Johnston, C. Gow and other skilful Artists.' Unlike the other studies presented here, these are not really histories or narratives, but vignettes, startling glimpses of the artistic representations of nineteenth century insanity. As such they reveal a vital but commonly concealed feature of case studies: the display of the mad, the forming of their ranks into an exhibition for the gratification of public curiosity.

The volume has no page numbers, but each written entry faces a numbered engraving. Some are given a heading indicating the type of insanity suffered, of which three examples are included here.

*Reprinted in 1976 by Arno Press, New York.

M. P. aged 40, a married woman; mother of nine children; in a state of mania of six months duration; the attack, which was not hereditary, was preceded by severe cough with expectoration, giving rise to a suspicion of impending Consumption of the Lungs – The Catamenia were irregular.

She knocked her head against the wall – broke whatever came in her way – talked incoherently of being great and rich – expressed fear of being murdered – swore – threatened her husband and mother – but retained her affection for her children.

Cathartics – two Setons in the neck; Leeches to the pudenda and Emmenagogues were employed without benefit.

E. E. L. aged 20. This Female, was seized with Puerperal Mania ten days after the birth of her second child, whom she had suckled for several days – her face was flushed, her eyes had a wild glistening appearance, and wandered rapidly from one object to another; she became very restless, tore her clothes, laid herself on the floor, knocked down her nurse, and required restraint; her conversation was incoherent, she talked of having thousands of children; she had no hereditary disposition to insanity.

E. I. aged 33. This Female, who had no hereditary disposition to insanity, was seized with Puerperal Mania three days after the birth of her first child; she is here represented eight weeks after the commencement of her disorder – her face pale, and her eyes and mouth shut; at times she is very silent, at other times she is very noisy, and screams; she attempted to jump out at a window, is disposed to tear her clothes, and frequently drops on her knees; her conversation is incoherent, sometimes she says that she is strange, that she is mad, that she shall destroy her child, or cut her own throat; restraint is found necessary.

EROTOMANIA
A. A., aged 25, a domestic servant.

In this patient the disorder at first assumed the form of Mania, but was very soon limited to amatory ideas, and these were directed towards the clergyman of her parish.

She is now (at the time this portrait was taken) very affectionate in her manner and generally disposed to kiss, but she never transgresses the bounds of decency in language; her face is flushed and her eyes are brilliant.

She has been in this state about four months.

EROTOMANIA

M. S. P. aged 22, an unmarried female, educated as a governess – had a hereditary tendency to insanity.

She was naturally of a very chaste and modest disposition; her Catamenia had been obstructed for six months, about three years age, and she became insane. Her insanity assumed a religious character, she conceived herself to be 'the Virgin Mary; that she had received spiritual birth on a certain day, for she then felt joy by the Holy Ghost;' she was quite cured after the disease had existed about a year, and she remained well for two years and a half.

She now labours under a second attack, and has been two months insane; she expresses her love for the clergyman whom she has attended; her eyes are red and brilliant, her face is flushed and her ideas are amatory, for she expresses a wish to be kissed – talks of being pregnant with something holy, and of marriage; but she does not farther transgress the bounds of decency in looks or discourse.

Portrait of A. S., aged 40, a married female; she is full of fear on many subjects – fears that she is changed into another person – that her husband is coming to harm – that she cannot get a livelihood – that she is passed all hope of salvation.

She is very noisy and restless, disturbing all around her, but sometimes ceases her cries for a moment, as if to listen to what is said; at times she appears to wish to speak, but stops short and says nothing.

This state had existed 18 months when her portrait was taken – it commenced on the sudden death of a favorite sister, who died in a state of delirium three days after delivery.

Cupping, Blisters, Andynes, Tonics, &c. were tried without effect, and the occurrence of numerous boils was not attended with any benefit.

M. E., aged 43, a married woman, without children, was deserted by her husband, which threw her into a state of low spirits for about a year, to which delirium was gradually joined; about ten weeks before her portrait was taken she made an attempt to drown herself, but appears not to have had courage to accomplish her design, for she was found in a large pool of water, where she had been standing several hours.

In this case much benefit was derived from the employment of purgative and tonic medicines.

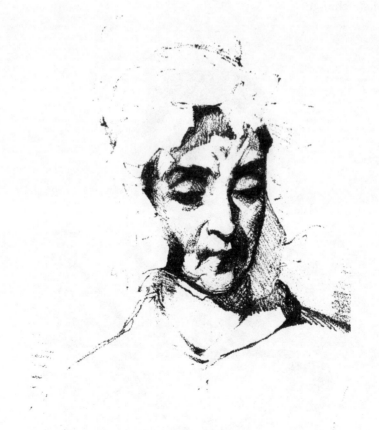

ACUTE DEMENTIA

Portrait of a female, in a state of Dementia, brought on suddenly, it is said, by having been violated.

She never spoke or moved; nothing attracted her attention; her usual posture was the one represented. She exemplified one of those continually-repeated automatic movements alluded to, called by French authors – *tic*; in her this was a slight smacking of the lips.

No remedies were of any avail, and she lately died in the Lunatic Asylum at Hanwell in a state of chronic Dementia, having remained several years from the first attack with very little change.

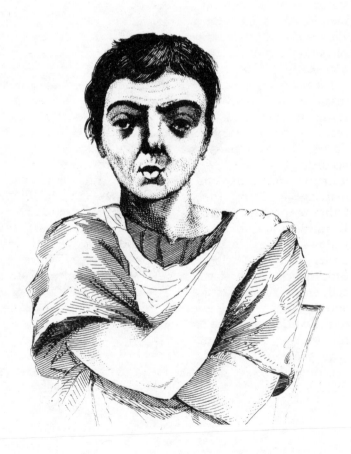

J. E. D. Esquirol, *Mental Maladies: A Treatise on Insanity*, translated with additions by E. K. Hunt (Philadelphia, 1845)

This work was originally published in Paris in 1838 as *Des Maladies Mentales Considérées sous les Rapports Medical, Hygienique et Médico-Legal*. A pupil of Pinel, Esquirol's writings were of considerable influence, and much discussed in England. In this work he speculated about the ratios of insane women to insane men by way of statistical tables of admissions to the Becêtre and Salpêtrière, suggesting that while women were more vulnerable in France, they were not in England because they received a better education. These statistics and their controversial reception are briefly mentioned in Chapter 2. When Morison (author of the *Phsyiognomy*) visited Esquirol, he noted that the French physician had 200 plastercasts of the faces of the insane, and 600 skulls.

Like Pinel, Esquirol stressed moral factors as causes of insanity, particularly in those kinds which he classified as forms of monomania. The extracts here are taken from the section titled 'Erotic Monomania', which concludes that the disease is 'essentially cerebral' and should be treated accordingly. Thus 'when amorous sentiments affect the nutritive functions, and threaten the life of the patient, marriage is almost the only efficacious remedy' (p. 342). Other treatments are also proposed. Elsewhere in this work Esquirol notes that he has often seen 'girls, and young widows, cured by marriage' and gives examples ('I understand, from a physician who has charge of the insane at Stockholm, that a young maniac, having escaped from his cell, enters the habitation of a young woman who is insane; and that, after having given themselves up during the night, to the wildest venereal transports, the former was found on the following morning dead, and the latter cured'). Unexpectedly he then states that he regards such instances as exceptional, and that marriage and pregnancy more frequently exacerbate insanity than cure it (pp. 195-6).

1. pp. 336–7

The following case is the more interesting, as it presents the characteristics of erotic delirium without complication. A lady thirty-two years of age, tall, of a strong constitution and nervous temperament, having blue eyes, a light complexion, and chestnut-coloured hair, had received her education at a school, in which the most brilliant future, and the highest pretensions were presented in perspective, to those young persons who went from this institution. Some time after her marriage, she saw a young man of a higher rank than her husband, and immediately becomes strongly impressed in his favour, though she had never spoken to him. She begins by complaining of her position, and speaking with contempt of her husband. She murmers at being obliged to live with him, and at length conceives an aversion for him, as well as her nearest relatives, who endeavor, in vain, to recall her from her error. The evil increases, and it becomes necessary to separate her from her husband. She goes into the family of her father, discourses constantly of the object of her passion, and becomes difficult, capricious and choleric. She also suffers from nervous pains. She escapes from the house of her relatives to pursue *him*. She sees him every where, and addresses him in passionate songs. He is the handsomest, the greatest, the most humorous, amiable and perfect of men. She never had any other husband. It is him who lives in her heart, controls its pulsations, governs her thoughts and actions, animates and adorns her existence. She is sometimes surprised in a kind of ecstasy, and ravished with delight. She is then motionless; her look is fixed, and a smile is upon her lips. She frequently writes letters and verses, copying them several times, with much care; and though they express the most vehement passion, are proof of the most virtuous sentiments. When she walks, she moves with sprightliness, and with the air of one engrossed in thought; or else her step is slow and haughty. She avoids men whom she disdains, and places far below her idol. However, she is not always indifferent to those marks of interest that are shown her; while every expression, that is not altogether respectful, offends her. To proofs of affection and devotion, she opposes the name, merit, and perfections of him whom she adores.

During both day and night, she often converses by herself; now, in a high, and now, in a low tone. She is now, gay and full of laughter; now, melancholic and weeps; and is now angry, in her solitary conversations. If any one refers to these, she assures him that she is constrained to speak. Most frequently it is her *lover who converses with her, by means known to himself alone.* She sometimes believes, that jealous persons endeavour to oppose her good fortune, by disturbing her conversation, and striking her. (I have seen her ready to break out into a violent paroxysm of fury, after having uttered a loud cry, assuring me that she has just been struck.) Under other circumstances, her face is flushed, and her eyes sparkling. She rages against every one, utters cries, and no longer recognizes the person with whom she lives. She is furious, and utters the most threatening language. This state, which is usually temporary, sometimes persists for two and three days, after which, the patient experiences violent pains at the epigastrium and heart. These pains, which are confined to the precordial region, and *which she could not endure without aid furnished by her lover, are caused by her relatives and friends, although they may be several leagues distant from her, or by persons who are about her.* The appearance of force, and words spoken with decision, restrain her. She then grows pale, and trembles; tears flow, and terminate the paroxysm.

This lady, who is rational in every other respect, labors, and carefully superintends the objects, which are adapted to her convenience and use. She does justice to the merit of her husband, and the tenderness of her relatives, but can neither see the former, nor live with the latter. The menses are regular and abundant; the paroxysms of excitement ordinarily taking place at the menstrual period, though not always. Her appetite is capricious, and her actions, like her language, are subordinate to the whims of her delirious passion. She sleeps little, and her rest is troubled by dreams, and even nightmare. She has long seasons of watchfulness, and when she does not sleep, walks about, talking to herself or singing. This disease was of several years' duration, when she was committed to my care. A systematic treatment for a year, isolation, tepid, cold and shower baths, antispasmodics externally and internally employed, none of them succeed in restoring to the use of her reason, this interesting patient.

2. pp. 338–9

A young female, with no apparent physical disease, without any known cause, becomes sad and thoughtful. The countenance assumes a pale hue, the eyes sink in their sockets, and the tears flow involuntarily. The sufferer experiences turns of prostration, without previous exertion; groans and sighs. Nothing diverts her, or engages her attention. On the contrary, every thing wearies her. She avoids her relatives and friends; and neither speaks nor replies to anyone. Her appetite is feeble, and capricious. She does not sleep; or, if she does, her rest is disturbed, and she becomes emaciated. Her relatives expect, by marriage, to restore her from this condition, which fills their minds with disquietude. She accepts, at first with indifference, the various proposals that are made to her. Shortly after however, she refuses them all with obstinacy. The malady continues to increase, and fever ensues. The pulse is irregular, disordered, and sometimes slow. Certain convulsive movements are observed, some thoughts irrationally expressed, and particularly certain strange actions. She finally sinks into marasmus, and dies. Death revealed the secret. Diffidence, an imperfect religious education, and the fear of displeasing her relatives, have determined her to conceal the emotions of her heart, and the true cause of her malady. . . .

This variety of erotomania is not rare. There are few physicians who have not had occasion to observe and propose a remedy for it; which is sometimes too late, when the disease has a very acute course. A young lady of Lyons falls in love with one of her relatives, to whom she was promised in marriage. Circumstances oppose the fulfillment of promises made to the two lovers, and the father requires the removal of the young man. He has scarcely gone, when this young lady falls into a state of profound sadness, says nothing, confines herself to her bed, refuses all nourishment, and the secretions become supressed. She repulses all the advice, prayers and consolations of her relatives and friends. After five days, vainly employed in endeavors to overcome her resolution, they decide on recalling her lover; but it was now too late. She sinks, and dies in his arms on the sixth day. I was struck with the rapid progress of his malady, in the case of a woman who died in seven days, after having established in her mind a conviction of the indifference of her husband.

3. pp. 340–1

Madeleine, at the age of fifteen years, is taken from the Foundling hospital, to the family of a country woman who, supposing that her only son had died in the army, adopts her as her daughter. Two years afterwards, her son returns. Soon, the pleasing person and cheerful disposition of Madeleine attract Jean-Pierre. On her part, she loves him with all her heart, she complies with his desires, and would have regarded herself as ungrateful, in refusing anything to the son of her mother by adoption. Three years pass in this tender intimacy, and with the expectation, on her part, of marrying Jean-Pierre. But he forsakes Madeleine, and marries another. This poor girl, in despair, loses her reason, wanders about the fields, and throws herself into the river, from whence she is taken, and sent to the Hôtel-Dieu. At the expiration of six weeks, she is transferred to the Salpêtrière, early in September. During the first year of her residence in the hospital, she suffers from erotic mania and fury, committing acts of violence upon her companions and herself. To this condition monomania succeeds, whose only object is Jean-Pierre, whom Madeleine loves, notwithstanding his infidelity. At her menstrual periods, her agitation is renewed, when this unhappy being is intractable, irascible and choleric. She is unceasingly calling for Jean-Pierre, often repeats his name, and says that no one is comparable with him. A calm, attended by a painful sadness, returns again, so soon as the menses cease to flow. Madeleine is habitually reserved and thoughtful, meditating upon her infidel lover. She performs some trifling services in the division for the insane, and if anything is said to her respecting young men, she regards it with disdain. She sings, and sometimes laughs and is very gay; at others, she weeps. She will ever love Jean-Pierre. Those who love sincerely, always love.

A lady eighty years of age, who, in her youth, had lived

amidst the illusions of the great, being reduced in her circumstances, to the income of a moderate fortune, spent her time in the country, and enjoyed excellent health, notwithstanding her advanced age. In consequence of the events of 1830, this lady is taken with erotomania. The object of her love is a young man, who has taken an active part in the affairs of this period. She believes that she is beloved, assures herself that her menses are again established, makes her toilet with much display, awaits her lover at the rendezvous, causes food to be prepared which she herself carries to the field, persuaded that the object of her attachment will come to partake of it with her. She hears him address her, she converses with him, sees him, and seeks for him everywhere. After some months, her brain becomes progressively enfeebled; and in one year after the manifestation of delirium, she sinks into dementia. She converses alone, and in a low tone; often pronouncing the name of the objects of her delirium.

Mad'e de L., of a nervous-sanguine temperament, a very vivid imagination, and educated on philosophical principles; having a decided taste for the reading of medical writings and romances, enjoyed excellent health, although very nervous and impressible. Reduced almost to penury by the revolution, which cost her husband his life upon the scaffold, she was constrained to form an establishment, to complete her means of subsistence, and secure a livelihood for her son, who only knew how to write bad verses.

She receives into her house a student of medicine, twenty-three years of age. She is at first well disposed towards this young man, but soon becomes prodigal of her attentions to him, and her civilities are exaggerated. At a later period, her carriage, her agitation, her impatience, her gayety and sadness, her thoughtless complaints, and ridiculous expenditures, betray the moral disorder under which this lady now labors, at the age of sixty-four years. This young man – though he little merits it – is ever the subject of her praise. She contemplates his future prospects, his successes and disappointments, more than her own affairs. The crosses and rude conduct; the evident causes of jealousy, and the indifference of the young student, who ridicules the

attachment of this superannuated female; the warnings and
advice of her devoted friends; the railery of persons who dwell
in the house, and the coarse pleasantries of the domestics; all
fail to bring back her lost reason, though, in every other
respect, she enjoys the respect of society, and performs with
spirit and propriety the honours of her house. However, she
does not sleep; her appetite is poor; and she becomes
emaciated. Never did she entertain the thought of seeking
happiness from the pleasures of sense. At the expiration of
two years, this student deserts the house; but this does not
undeceive her. She not only excuses his clandestine flight, but
the serious wrongs and baseness which it reveals. She loves
still. She remains for several months, very much depressed in
mind, and at length falls into a state of complete
wretchedness, and dies eight years subsequently, from a
cancer of the uterus.

This case presents a remakable feature; since, at the age of
sixty-four years, when the erotic affection burst forth, the
patient menstruated regularly and abundantly for two years;
experiencing no interruption of the menses, but from the
grief which she suffered, in consequence of the departure of
the student. Was the cancer of the uterus, the effect of the
cessation of this late menstruation; or rather, was the nervous
irritation of the uterus, which so often precedes organic
lesions, the prime cause of the erotic delirium?

Select Bibliography

Full details of all primary and secondary texts quoted or referred to will be found in the footnotes. The following is a list of secondary texts that have been particularly useful in the preparation of this book, or bear some close relation to its concerns.

Auerbach, Nina, *Woman and the Demon: the life of a Victorian Myth*, Cambridge, Mass. and London, 1982.

Averill, James H., *Wordsworth and the Poetry of Human Suffering*, Ithaca and London, 1980.

Barthes, Roland, *Mythologies*, trans. by Annette Lavers, London, 1973.

——, *Image–Music–Text*, trans. by Stephen Heath, London, 1977.

Butler, Marilyn, *Jane Austen and the War of Ideas*, Oxford, 1975.

Byrd, Max, *Visits to Bedlam: Madness and Literature in the Eighteenth Century*, Columbia, 1974.

Calder, Jenni, *Women and Marriage in Victorian Fiction*, London, 1976.

Deporte, Michael V., *Nightmares and Hobbyhorses: Swift, Sterne, and Augustan Ideas of Madness*, San Marino, 1974.

Derrida, Jacques, *Of Grammatology*, trans. by Gayatri Chakravorty Spivak, Baltimore and London, 1976.

Digby, Anne, *Madness, Morality and Medicine: A Study of the York Retreat, 1796–1914*, Cambridge, 1986.

Feder, Lilian, *Madness in Literature*, Princeton, 1980.

Felman, Shoshana, 'Women and Madness: The Critical Phallacy', *Diacritics*, 5 (1975), No. 4, 2–10.

Foucault, Michel, *Madness and Civilization: A History of Insanity in the Age of Reason*, trans. by Richard Howard, London, 1971.

————, *The Birth of the Clinic: An Archaeology of Medical Perception*, trans. by A. M. Sheridan, London, 1976.

————, *Discipline and Punish: The Birth of the Prison*, trans. by Alan Sheridan, London, 1976.

Galdston, Iago, 'Freud and Romantic Medicine', in *Freud: Modern Judgements*, ed. by Frank Cioffi, London, 1973.

Gallop, Jane, *Feminism and Psychoanalysis: The Daughter's Seduction*, London, 1982.

Gilbert, Sandra M. and Susan Gubar, *The Madwoman in the Attic: The Woman Writer and the Nineteenth Century Literary Imagination*, New Haven and London, 1979.

Glen, Heather, *Vision and Disenchantment: Blake's Songs and Wordsworth's Lyrical Ballads*, Cambridge, 1983.

Grange, Kathleen M., 'Pinel and Eighteenth Century Psychiatry', *Bulletin of the History of Medicine*, 35 (1961), 442–53.

Hagstrum, Jean, *Sex and Sensibility: Ideal and Erotic Love from Milton to Mozart*, Chicago, 1980.

Hunter, Richard and Ida Macalpine (eds), *Three Hundred Years of Psychiatry, 1535–1860*.

Jacobus, Mary, *Tradition and Experiment in Wordsworth's Lyrical Ballads (1798)*, Oxford, 1976.

Johnson, Barbera, *The Critical Difference*, Baltimore and London, 1980.

Jordan, John E., *Why the Lyrical Ballads?*, Berkeley and London, 1976.

Levinson, Marjorie, *Wordsworth's Great Period Poems*, Cambridge, 1986.

Marcus, Steven, 'Freud and Dora: Story, History, Case History', in Edith Kurzweil and William Phillips (eds), *Literature and Psychoanalysis*, New York, 1983.

Masters, Anthony, *Bedlam*, London, 1977.

Mayo, Robert, 'The Contemporaneity of the *Lyrical Ballads*', *PMLA*, 69 (1954), 486–522.

McGann, Jerome J., *The Romantic Ideology: A Critical Investigation*, Chicago and London, 1983.

Mitchell, Juliet, *Psychoanalysis and Feminism*, Harmondsworth, 1975.

Modleski, Tania, *Loving with a Vengeance: Mass-Produced Fantasies for Women*, New York and London, 1984.

Moglen, Helene, *Charlotte Brontë: The Self-Conceived*, New York, 1976.

Okin, Susan Moller, *Women in Western Political Thought*, London, 1980.

Rosen, George M., 'Romantic Medicine: A Problem in Historical

Periodization', *Bulletin of the History of Medicine*, 25 (1951), 149–58.

————, 'Emotion and Sensibility in Ages of Anxiety: A Comparative Historical Review', *American Journal of Psychiatry*, 124 (1967), 771–84.

Scull, Andrew T., *Museums of Madness: The Social Organization of Insanity in Nineteenth Century England*, Harmondsworth, 1982.

Showalter, Elaine, *A Literature of their Own: British Women Novelists from Brontë to Lessing*, Princeton, 1977.

Siefert, Susan, *The Dilemma of the Talented Heroine: A Study in Nineteenth Century Fiction*, Montreal, 1978.

Simpson, David, *Wordsworth and the Figurings of the Real*, London, 1982.

Skultans, Vieda, *Madness and Morals*, London, 1975.

————, *English Madness: Ideas of Insanity, 1580–1890*, London, 1979.

Slater, Michael, *Dickens and Women*, London, 1983.

Stone, Harry, *Dickens and the Invisible World: Fairy Tales, Fantasy, and Novel-Making*, London, 1980.

Stone, Lawrence, *Family, Sex, and Marriage in England, 1500–1800*, London, 1977.

Sulloway, Frank, *Freud, Biologist of the Mind*, London, 1979.

Szasz, Thomas, *The Manufacture of Madness*, London, 1971.

Veith, Ilza, *Hysteria: The History of a Disease*, Chicago and London, 1965.

Wordsworth, Jonathan, *The Music of Humanity: A Critical Study of Wordsworth's Ruined Cottage*, London, 1969.

Wright, Elizabeth, *Psychoanalytic Criticism: Theory and Practice*, London and New York, 1984.

Zeman, Anthea, *Presumptuous Girls: Women and their World in the Serious Woman's Novel*, London, 1977.

Index

Allen, M., *Essay on the
Classification of the Insane*,
172–5
Althusser, Louis, 'Marxism
and Humanism', 13
Arnold, Thomas, *Observations
on the Nature, Kinds, Causes
and Prevention, of Insanity*,
2, 31–2, 39, 40–1
Austen, Jane, *Sense and
Sensibility*, 4, 92–123 *passim*
Averill, James, *Wordsworth
and the poetry of Human
Suffering*, 10, 72, 90, 91

Barker, Thomas (Barker of
Bath), 27
Barlow, John *On Man's Power
over himself to prevent or
control Insanity*, 34–5
Barthes, Roland, 145;
Mythologies, 13
Bovary, Madame, 5
Breuer, Josef, 43, 140–1,
146–8, 158–60, 167
Brontë, Charlotte, 12; *Jane
Eyre*, 4, 7, 8, 9, 124–39
passim, 157–8; *Villette*, 5
Brontë, Emily, *Wuthering
Heights*, 4, 92–123 *passim*

Brydges, Sir Samual
Edgerton, *Mary de Clifford*,
25–6
Burrows, George Man,
*Commentaries on the Causes,
Forms, Symptoms and
Treatment . . . of Insanity*,
35; *An Inquiry into Certain
Errors relative to Insanity*,
36
Burton, Thomas, 89
Butler, James, 90, 91
Byrd, Max, *Visits to Bedlam*,
26

Carter, Robert Brudenell, *On
the Pathology and Treatment
of Hysteria*, 39–40
Cassandra, 15
Charcott, J.-M., 140, 160
Chilmead, Edmund, 1
Cixous, Hélène, *La jeune née*,
167–8
Coleridge, Samuel Taylor, 90
Collins, Wilkie, 6
Connolly, John, *An Inquiry
Concerning the Indications of
Insanity*, 30, 34
Cowper, William, *The Task*, 3,
19–22, 55, 58, 60, 70

Culler, Jonathan, *On Deconstruction*, 13

Dacre, Charlotte, 27
Danby, Francis, *Disappointed Love*, 95
Darwin, Erasmus, *Zoonomia; or, the Laws of Organic Life*, 2, 12, 37, 38, 40
De Beauvoir, Simone, 47
Derrida, Jacques, 8; *Of Grammatology*, 13
Dickens, Charles, 4, 10, 84, 92–123 *passim*, 127
Digby, Anne, *Madness, Morality and Medicine*, 13

Ellis, Sir William, *A Treatise on the Nature, Symptoms, Causes and Treatment of Insanity*, 29–30, 38, 169–72

Feder, Lilian, *Madness in Literature*, 26
Felman, Shoshana, 47
Ferrand, Jacques, 1
Fleiss, Wilhelm, 141
Foucault, Michel, 6, 11, 14, 30, 41–2; *Discipline and Punish*, 13; *The Birth of the Clinic*, 13; *Madness and Civilization*, 123
Fox, Charles James, 53, 87
Frankenstein, Dr, 163
Freud, Sigmund, 4, 5, 10, 16, 43, 64–5, 103–6, 111–12; 'Fragment of an Analysis of a Case of Hysteria', 142, 167; 'The Psychotherapy of Hysteria', 147, 160; *Studies on Hysteria*, 140–68 *passim*
Fuseli, Henry, ix, 19, 26

Gladston, Iago, 141
Gallop, Jane, *Feminism and Psychoanalysis*, 168
Gilbert, Sandra, and Gubar, Susan, *The Madwoman in the Attic*, 93, 126, 128, 129, 139
Gill, Stephen, 58, 90
Godwin, William, 12
Goodman, Alice, 91
Gramsci, Antonio, 13
Grange, Kathleen M., 12

Hardy, Thomas, 6
Hartley, David, *Observations on Man, his Frame, his Duty and his Expectations*, 37–8, 46
Harvey, William, 46
Haslam, John, *Observations on Insanity*, 31, 46
Helme, Elisabeth, 27
Hunter, Richard, and Macalpine, Ida, *Three Hundred Years of Psychiatry*, 12, 46, 47

Irigaray, Luce, 47, 94, 122
Isaacs, Mrs, 27

Jacobus, Mary, 64
Johnson, Barbera, 145
Jones, Ernest, *Sigmund Freud, Life and Work*, 168

Klein, Malanie, 126, 139

Lacan, Jacques, 94, 139
Lamb, Charles, 90
Lamb, Mary, ix
Lear, King, 14, 21, 59
Lee, Sophia, 27
Levinson, Marjorie, 10, 51, 90

Lewis, Matthew, *The Monk*, 107

Lister, Raymond, *Victorian Narrative Paintings*, 123

Lukács, Georg, 51

Mackenzie, Henry, *The Man of Feeling*, 17–22

Marcus, Stephen, 142

Mayo, Robert, 26, 27

McGann, Jerome J., 51

Mitchell, Juliet, *Psychoanalysis and Feminism*, 168

Moglen, Helena, *Charlotte Brontë: The Self-Conceived*, 139

Monthly Magazine or British Register, The, 23–4

Morison, Sir Alexander, *Outlines of Lectures on the Nature . . . of Insanity*, 29, 39, 176; *The Physiognomy of Mental Diseases*, 176–84, 185

Ophelia, 15

Pinel, Philippe, 2, 3, 4, 17, 172, 185

Plato, 14

Poe, Edgar Allen, 144–5

Pope, Alexander, *The Rape of the Lock*, 89; *Moral Essays*, 100

Reeve, Clara, 27

Rhys, Jean, *Wide Sargasso Sea*, 4, 7, 8, 93, 124–39 passim

Rosen George, 12, 48, 141

Sarratt, J. H., 27

Schelling, Friedrich, 43, 140

Scots Magazine, The, 22–3

Scott, Sir Walter, *The Bride of Lammermoor*, 4, 10, 92–123 passim

Shepheard, George, 19

Shuttleworth, Sally, 12

Siefert, Susan, 129–30

Skultans, Vieda, *English Madness*, 12, 48, 91; *Madness and Morals*, 46, 47

Southey, Robert, 25; 'The Complaints of the Poor', 25; 'Hannah', 25, 57, 90; 'Mary, the Maid of the Inn', 25, 57, 90; 'The Ruined Cottage', 25, 57, 90

Stone, Harry, *Dickens and the Invisible World*, 123

Stone, Lawrence, *Family, Sex and Marriage in England, 1500–1800*, 52

Sulloway, Frank J., *Freud, Biologist of the Mind*, 168

Sydenham, Thomas, 48

Szasz, Thomas S., *The Manufacture of Madness*, 26

Tennyson, Alfred Lord, 6

Trotter, Thomas, *A View of the Nervous Temperament*, 2, 32–4, 38–9

Tuke, Samuel, 172; *A Description of the Retreat*, 12

Veith, Ilza, *Hysteria, The History of a Disease*, 26, 47, 166

William, W. F., 27

Wordsworth, Jonathan, 79, 91

Wordsworth, William, 3–5, 9–12, 24, 49–91, 141; 'Affliction of Margaret,

The', 53; 'Anecdote for Fathers', 62; 'Baker's Cart, The', 80–2; *Borderers, The*, 57; 'Complaint of the Forsaken Indian Woman, The', 57, 63; 'Emigrant Mother, The', 57; 'Evening Walk, An', 57, 63; *Excursion, The*, 78, 83–6; 'Female Vagrant, The', 56, 58–69, 77; 'Forsaken, The', 57; *Guilt and Sorrow*, 56, 58; 'Her Eyes are Wild', 53, 65, 69; 'Incipient Madness', 80–2; *Lyrical Ballads, The*, 56, 62, 69–91 *passim*; 'Maternal Grief', 57; 'Old Cumberland Beggar, The', 68; *Preface to the Lyrical Ballads*, 62, 88; *Ruined Cottage, The*, 11, 53, 57, 69, 77–91 *passim*; 'Ruth', 53, 57, 63, 65–9, 87; 'Sailor's Mother, The', 53, 57, 75–7; *Salisbury Plain*, 53–91 *passim*; 'Tale, A', 55, 'Thorn, The', 53, 70–7, 87, 89; 'We are Seven', 62; 'Widow on Windermere's Side, The', 57

Wright, Elizabeth, *Psychoanalytic Criticism*, 139

Yeats, W. B., 5